It's Perfectly Normal

Changing Bodies, Growing Up, Sex, Gender, and Sexual Health

PRAISE FOR
It's Perfectly Normal

An American Library Association Notable Children's Book

A *Booklist* Editors' Choice

A *Boston Globe–Horn Book* Honor Winner

A *Bulletin of the Center for Children's Books* Blue Ribbon Winner

A *Horn Book* Best Book of the Year

A New York Public Library 100 Titles for Reading and Sharing Selection

A *New York Times Book Review* Notable Book of the Year

A *Parenting* Reading Magic Award Winner

A *Publishers Weekly* Best Children's Book of the Year

A *School Library Journal* Best Book of the Year

★ "A wonderful guide for young adolescents setting sail on the stormy seas of puberty."
—*School Library Journal* (starred review)

★ "Caring, conscientious, and well-crafted."
—*Booklist* (starred review)

★ "Intelligent, amiable, and carefully researched."
—*Publishers Weekly* (starred review)

★ "One of the most unintimidating and informative sex books to come along for this age group."
—*Bulletin of the Center for Children's Books* (recommended and starred review)

★ "A terrific teaching tool that just may help slow the spread of sexual disease and ignorance."
—*Kirkus Reviews* (starred review)

★ "The book will serve as a useful tool in the sex education curriculum." —*The Horn Book* (starred review)

"Informal, wide-ranging, candid, and funny. . . . A younger child can enjoy the art. . . . An independent reader can seek definitions in privacy. Preadolescents can test their knowledge. And adolescents can give a superior smirk while secretly learning what they most need to know about sexual survival." —*The New York Times Book Review*

"A family-friendly guide to everything your kids ever asked you about sex, but you were afraid to answer."
—*Child* Magazine

"Reliable basic information is provided about both the mechanics and the consequences of puberty, sexual activity, birth control, pregnancy, and sexually transmitted diseases." —*Parenting*

"Utterly contemporary and comprehensive. . . . Highly recommended for talking your way through just about any embarrassing interrogation your ever-curious kids can devise." —*Los Angeles Times Book Review*

"A frank and funny compendium that includes unbiased and up-to-date information . . . all explained in jaunty and accurate full-color art depicting people of many races, cultures, sizes, and ages."
—*San Francisco Chronicle Book Review*

"*It's Perfectly Normal* answers more pre-adolescent questions about sex than any others on the shelf, and it does it gently, scientifically, and with humor."
—*The Press-Enterprise*, Riverside County, California

"Conversations with kids about sex are about as welcome by most parents as dental surgery. . . . Robie H. Harris has made it easier with *It's Perfectly Normal*. . . . The book, for ages 10 and up, is sophisticated, comprehensive, reassuring." —*USA Today*

PRAISE FROM THE EXPERTS

"*It's Perfectly Normal* gives growing children a chance to read an honest and explanatory view of their developing bodies. The text and pictures will give them a chance to understand and value themselves. I recommend it to parents, children, and adolescents. They will love it!"
—**T. Berry Brazelton, MD, founder of Brazelton Touchpoints Center, Boston Children's Hospital, and Joshua Sparrow, MD, co-authors of *Touchpoints: Birth to Three* and *Touchpoints: Three to Six*, Boston, MA**

"*It's Perfectly Normal*, as well as Harris and Emberley's books for younger children, are some of the best tools available to promote family communication about critical topics related to sexuality. We know from research that when families communicate about sexual and reproductive health topics, preteens and teens make healthier decisions. *It's Perfectly Normal* will spur parent-child communication about essential topics like puberty, sex, relationships, sexual orientation, gender identity, and more. In today's world, where young people are bombarded with messages from many sources, having this carefully crafted, age-appropriate, and engaging book is a gift to us all."
—**Leslie M. Kantor, PhD, MPH, professor and chair, Department of Urban-Global Public Health, Rutgers School of Public Health, Newark, NJ; former vice president of education, Planned Parenthood Federation of America, New York, NY**

"*It's Perfectly Normal* remains one of the most useful, accessible, and inclusive resources for talking with youth and families about sex, gender, relationships, and values. These conversations help young people learn how to make safe and healthy choices and live their lives with integrity. *It's Perfectly Normal* is the perfect catalyst to start these conversations."
—**Melanie Davis, MEd, PhD, CSC, CSE, Our Whole Lives program manager, Unitarian Universalist Association, Boston, MA**

"If you have ever found it difficult to talk to your child about sex, or even if you find it easy, this book will be an invaluable friend. The quality of the information it provides is superb. Its language and illustrations speak in a direct, nonjudgmental manner and present diverse families, diverse relationships, and diverse bodies.

Harris and Emberley cover everything a young person needs to know about sexual health, including how to safely use the Internet by providing strategies for finding reliable information and ways to prevent potential hazards of Internet use. It will draw in tweens, teens, and parents and totally engage all."
—**Angela Diaz, MD, MPH, Jean C. and James W. Crystal Professor, Departments of Pediatrics and of Preventative Medicine, Icahn School of Medicine at Mount Sinai; director, Mount Sinai Adolescent Health Center, New York, NY**

"Now more than ever, America's preteens and teens in every community across our nation need the latest and most accurate information about sexual health as they go through the challenging ups and downs of puberty and adolescence. *It's Perfectly Normal* is the go-to book for every young person. Why? Because it educates our youth about sexuality in the most honest and respectful manner and does not shy away from giving them the very information they are looking for and need."
—**Marc H. Morial, president and CEO, National Urban League, Inc., New York, NY**

"At last! A book that tells preteens and teenagers what they need to know about sex without turning off the less sophisticated, turning on the more sophisticated, or offending the moral values or sensibilities of parents and teachers. *It's Perfectly Normal* is informative and interesting; reassuring and responsible; warm and charming. I wish every child (and parent) could have a copy."
—**Penelope Leach, PhD, author of *Your Baby & Child* and *Children First*, London, England**

A Note to the Reader

Ever since *It's Perfectly Normal* was first published twenty-five+ years ago, we have never stopped talking with older kids, preteens, teens, and adults about the information and issues in this book. This has given us the chance to learn even more about what you need to know to stay healthy. We are so excited to share our newest and the most fully updated edition of this book with you. This edition is jam-packed with the latest information kids and teens need to know to stay healthy and safe.

Over the years, we have also continued to ask experts, including parents, teachers, librarians, doctors, nurses, psychologists, psychoanalysts, scientists, and clergy, what information about puberty, sex, sexual health, and gender needs to be changed, updated, or added to keep you healthy.

Whenever changes in the text and the art are necessary to make this book as up-to-date and accurate as possible, we make them. For this edition, we have updated the scientific and medical information and have added more information and facts about gender, reproduction, birth control, abortion, sexual abuse, sexually transmitted diseases, and many other topics.

Since so many of you use cell phones, tablets, and computers to go online to find information and to communicate with others, we have added more information and facts about the benefits and risks of being online. We believe this will help you use the Internet to find truthful,

accurate, responsible, and up-to-date information about sexual health and will help you protect your own as well as your friends' and your family's privacy and personal safety.

While writing and illustrating this book, we checked and rechecked the scientific information and the latest research. We learned from scientists and health professionals that knowledge about this subject is continually evolving and changing. While there is much agreement, there is also some disagreement, and some questions still remain. At this time, the information in this book is as up-to-date and as accurate as possible. If you have more questions or need further information, most always it can be very helpful to talk with someone you know and can trust—a parent, doctor, nurse, teacher, school counselor, therapist, or clergyperson.

Today, even more kids have a chance to read *It's Perfectly Normal*. It has been translated into more than thirty-five languages and is read around the world—from the United States to the United Kingdom, Denmark, the Netherlands, Germany, Italy, Spain, Poland, Japan, China, Mongolia, South Africa, and Australia.

We hope that our newest edition will help to keep you healthy and safe. We also hope it will help you and your friends make informed and responsible decisions about sexual health as you continue to grow up and go through puberty and adolescence.

Robie H. Harris and Michael Emberley

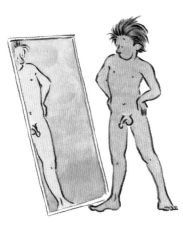

It's
Perfectly
Normal

Changing Bodies, Growing Up,
Sex, Gender, and Sexual Health

ROBIE H. HARRIS

illustrated by
MICHAEL EMBERLEY

CANDLEWICK PRESS

Contents

INTRODUCTION
Lots of Questions

Changing Bodies, Growing Up, Sex, Gender, and Sexual Health

Sometime between the ages of eight or nine and fifteen or so, kids' bodies begin to change and grow into adult bodies.

> Gr-r-reat!

> Gr-r-ross!

Most kids wonder about and have lots of questions about what will be happening to them as their bodies change and grow during this time.

> Not me.

> Me.

It's perfectly normal for kids to be curious about and want to know about their changing and growing bodies. Most of the changes—but not all—that take place during this time make it possible for humans to make a baby and give birth to a baby. And making a baby has a lot to do with sex.

> Well, I do know that this stuff is not just about the birds and the bees.

> It's about the facts of life.

Sex is about a lot of things—bodies, growing up, families, babies, love, caring, curiosity, feelings, respect, responsibility, biology, and health. There are times when sickness and danger can be a part of sex, too.

Most kids wonder about and have lots of questions about sex. It's also perfectly normal to want to know about sex.

> Whew! I was feeling weird.

> I was feeling perfectly normal.

You may wonder why it's a good idea to learn some facts about bodies, about growing up, about sex, about sexual health, and also about gender. It's important because these facts can help you stay healthy, take good care of yourself, and make good decisions about yourself as you are growing up and for the rest of your life.

Besides, learning about these things can be fascinating and fun.

> Doesn't sound like that much fun to me.

> Maybe you *are* weird.

PART ONE
What Is Sex?

1
Babies, Kids, Preteens, Teens, Grown-ups
Sex and Gender

What is sex? What is it . . . exactly? What is it all about?

These are questions lots of kids wonder about. You needn't feel embarrassed or stupid if you don't know the answers, because sex is not a simple matter.

Sex is many things, and people have many different feelings and opinions about it. That's why there is more than one answer to the question, What is sex?

One way to find out about sex is to ask someone you know and trust. Remember, there are no stupid questions. Another way to find out about sex is to read about it. For example, you can look up the meaning of the word *sex* in the dictionary. Here is what one dictionary says under the word *sex*:

1: *Either of the two groups, female or male, into which most living things are placed.*

2: *A label usually given at birth to humans and other living things based solely on the male body parts or the female body parts they have or were born with.*

Looking up words such as *sex* or *gender* or other words in a dictionary can be a good way to find helpful information. But some dictionaries may not have the most up-to-date information. And other dictionaries

Sex is not just any old hugging and kissing. And it's not just about love. I know that much.

Well, it's not just making babies, either.

IT'S PERFECTLY NORMAL

may not include everything you may want to or need to know about sex or gender. There is a lot to learn about sex and about gender.

Sex is in the dictionary!

Yep, *sex* is a word, and words are in dictionaries.

Most people want to know the sex of a new baby. So it's no surprise that—even if the parent or parents knew the sex of the baby before birth—the moment a baby is born, someone will often shout out, "It's a girl!" or "It's a boy!"

And often one of the questions kids may wonder about or ask when they first hear that a new kid is joining their class is, "Is it a boy or a girl?" When kids ask that question, they are usually asking about a person's sex. The labels "girl," "boy," "male," and "female" are labels that most babies are given at birth. But these labels are only based on what the parent, doctor, nurse, or midwife sees at the moment of birth. If that

baby has a penis, most often the baby is labeled "boy." And if that baby has a vagina, most often the baby is labeled "girl." However, not all people's bodies, including babies' bodies, are exactly the same. Most babies are born with either a vagina or a penis. Some babies are born with a mixture of male body parts and female body parts. If a person is born with that mixture, their sex is "intersex," which is the word that is often used to describe that mixture.

When people talk about sex and body parts, many think they are talking about a person's gender. But gender is not just about our body parts. Gender is also about the many thoughts and feelings each of us has about being who we are: a girl or a boy, or a man or a woman, or a mixture of genders, or somewhere between female and male, or neither male nor female.

Many people use the words *girl* or *boy*, or *man* or *woman*, to describe who they are. Yet other people feel or know that those words do not describe who they are and that the sex they were assigned at birth does not fit with who they are.

They may be or feel that they are a different gender than the gender they were assigned at birth. Or they may feel that neither female nor male describes who they are and may not want to use *girl* or *boy*, *man* or *woman*, or *female* or *male* to describe who they are. Other people choose not to be defined by their gender. They feel that there are more things than gender that define who they are.

A baby's birth certificate, which is a record of a baby's birth, usually has two genders listed on it—female or male. There are some states and cities that have now added another option for gender to their birth certificates—the gender X. This means that parents in those states or cities may record "female" or "male" or "X" (after the word "sex," that is) on their baby's birth certificate at birth. Parents in these states and cities also have the option of changing their child's gender on their birth certificate at a later date in their child's life. Older children in some of these states and cities also have the option of changing their own gender on their birth certificate at a later date in their lives.

How you feel, see, and describe yourself—whether it is according to the sex you were assigned at birth or the gender you now feel and know you are—is called your gender identity. A person's gender identity is often defined by the clothes we wear, or by the way we behave, or by the way we look, or by other traits we may have.

Sometimes other people may try to define your gender for you. But who you are is most always the person you feel you are, or figure out you are, or already know you are, no matter what anyone else may say or think about you.

Gender is many things. That's why there is more than one answer to the question, What is gender?

Hey, now I know about sex AND gender!

Hey, now I don't need to know ANYTHING else about that stuff!

CERTIFICATE OF BIRTH

NAME OF CHILD

DATE AND TIME OF CHILD'S BIRTH

PLACE OF CHILD'S BIRTH

PARENT(S) NAME

RESIDENCE

GENDER ☐ MALE ☐ FEMALE ☐ X

APPROVED
Evelyn Norman
April 5, 2021

2
Making Babies
Sexual Reproduction

The dictionary tells us more about sex. It says,

3: *Sexual reproduction.*

Sex is also about reproduction—making babies. *To reproduce* means to "produce again," or "make again."

When our bodies have grown up and become adult bodies, certain parts of our bodies make it possible to reproduce—to make babies. The parts of our bodies that make this possible are called the reproductive organs.

Our bodies' organs are the parts of our bodies that have special jobs to perform. For example, the heart is the organ whose special job is to pump blood. Scientists know that most organs inside our bodies,

such as our hearts, our lungs, and our stomachs, are the same no matter what sex or gender we are. One group of organs that is not the same for female bodies and male bodies is the reproductive organs.

People also call the reproductive organs the sexual organs or the sex organs. Our sex organs are designed to work in an amazingly interesting way. They are different from each other because they have different jobs to do.

Babies, kids, teens, and adults all have outer sex organs and inner sex organs. Some are located between our legs, on the outside of our bodies. The sex organs on the outside of a person's body are often called the genitals. Some of our sex organs are located inside our bodies. The sex organs inside a person's body are called the reproductive organs.

People have different sex organs. Some people have a vagina and ovaries. Some people have a penis and

testicles. Some people have a mixture of male and female sex organs.

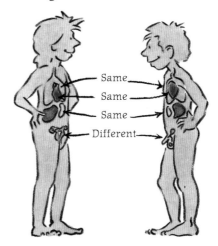

When the phrase *sex organs* is used in these ways, people are usually talking about our bodies' reproductive organs, which are the parts of our bodies that can make a new human being—make a baby.

3
Strong Feelings
Sexual Desire

The dictionary tells us even more about sex. It says,

4: *Sexual desire.*

Sex is also the desire to be physically close to someone, as close as you can be.

Do you ever really want or crave something? That's desire, like when you really want someone to be your best friend or when you really want chocolate ice cream.

I prefer strawberry ice cream.

I'm a chocolate freak myself.

You don't know why you want these things. You don't even think about why you want them. These are simply feelings of wanting—of desire.

Sexual desire is different from these desires—different from just wanting chocolate ice cream, or wanting someone to be your best friend, or even wanting to snuggle up to your parent, a friend, a pet, or a stuffed animal.

Sexual desire means you feel attracted to someone in a very strong way . . . like being pulled by a magnet. You want to be as physically close to that person as you can be.

Even though you may think about that person a lot, sexual desire is mostly the way you feel in your body about that person. Your body may feel excited or warm or quivery or tingly. And sometimes these feelings can be very strong.

For lots of kids, sexual desire can happen when one has happy, nervous, or exciting feelings about another person— feelings that you may even feel inside your body. Often it's hard to stop thinking about that person and you may even think you are in love with that person. That's called "having a crush" on someone. Having crushes is perfectly normal. Not having crushes is also perfectly normal.

Many, but not all, kids have crushes. Kids may have crushes on people they know, as well as on people they don't know—like TV stars, movie stars, rap stars, rock stars, or sports stars.

Kids may have crushes on people who are the same gender they are or who are a different gender, on people who are the same age they are, or who are older, or younger.

The feelings and thoughts you may have about other people and their bodies can make you feel very excited. Some people call this "feeling sexy."

Some of you are probably noticing the changes in your own bodies and the differences between your body and your friends' bodies. Sex can also be about the many new thoughts and feelings you may have about what's happening to you and your body as you are growing up.

I don't have any crushes ...on anybody!

Not true. You have crushes on a zillion rock stars. You've got posters of The Beetles and The Creepy Cockroaches and The Hairy Tarantulas all over your beehive.

4
Making Love
Sexual Intercourse

The dictionary tells us one more thing about sex. It says,

5: *Sexual intercourse.*

Sex can also mean sexual intercourse. Some people call sexual intercourse "having sex."

Now we're getting to IT!

Getting to WHAT?

Oh, never mind. I wonder if you can find out even more about sex in the encyclopedia. . . .

Most often, sexual intercourse happens when two people feel very sexy and very attracted to each other and may also have very loving and romantic feelings about each other. These feelings often make them want to or decide to be very close to each other in a sexual way. People can have these feelings for people of a different gender, or for people of the same gender, or for all genders.

One kind of sexual intercourse happens when a person with a female body and a person with a male body are so close to each other that the penis goes inside the vagina, and the vagina stretches in a

way that fits around the penis. This kind of touching can make the whole body feel good—feel sexy. And when this kind of sexual intercourse happens, it is possible for a female body and a male body—once their reproductive organs have grown up—to make a baby.

This is what I thought IT was about.

I'd rather not think about IT.

Most people don't have sexual intercourse only when

they want a baby. Most often, people have sexual intercourse because it feels good. People have sexual intercourse well into old age.

When a couple has sexual intercourse and does not want to make a baby, there are healthy ways, called birth control, that can help keep them from making a baby or from passing on an infection to one another.

Sometimes, a couple does not plan ahead or decide whether or not to have sexual intercourse. Planning ahead is most often the most effective way to keep a pregnancy from beginning.

People also call sexual intercourse "making love" or "lovemaking" because it's a way of expressing love. But sexual intercourse is only one way of expressing love.

Another kind of sexual intercourse happens when the sexual parts of two people who have female bodies touch or when the sexual parts of two people who have male bodies touch. This kind of touching can make the whole body feel good—feel sexy. Since male bodies have only sperm cells and no egg cells—and since female bodies have only egg

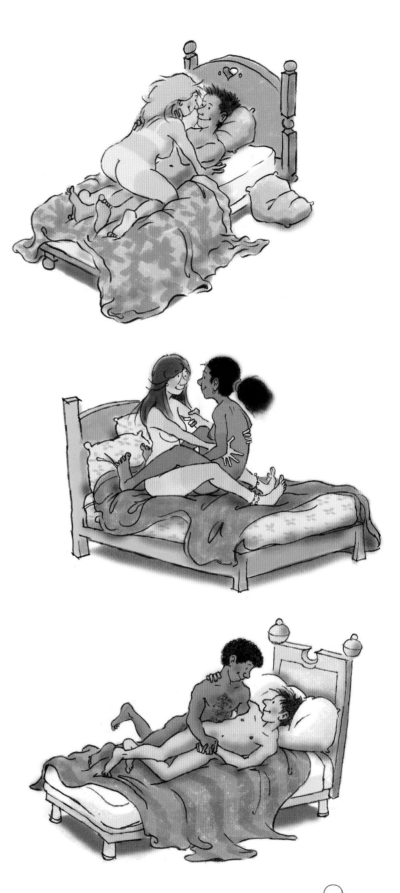

cells and no sperm cells—the beginning cells of a baby cannot start to grow and a pregnancy cannot begin when two people of the same sex have sexual intercourse.

Hugging, cuddling, holding hands, kissing, and touching are other ways of expressing love. So is just being with someone you like a lot and telling that person, "I love you."

There are some things about sex and sexual intercourse that are important to know and remember:

- It makes sense to wait to have sexual intercourse until you are old enough and responsible enough to make healthy decisions about sex.
- Every person, no matter what their gender or how young or old they are, has the right to say no to any kind of touching—even when one person is older, or a lot older, or stronger, or a lot stronger than the other person.
- A relationship that includes sexual contact often comes with exciting and good feelings. But sometimes, it may come with complicated feelings.
- Sexual intercourse—"having sex"—can involve the penis and the vagina, or the mouth

and the genitals, or the penis and the anus.

- After sexual intercourse that involves the vagina and the penis, a pregnancy can begin. But there are many ways a person can protect oneself from becoming pregnant and having a baby.
- During sexual intercourse, serious infections such as HPV, a virus that can cause some kinds of cancer, and HIV, the virus that causes AIDS, as well as other infections that are serious and others that are less serious, can be passed from one person to the other. Some are very hard to cure and others are easier to cure. However, there are ways in which people can help protect themselves from getting or passing on these infections.
- Not every person will want to or choose to have sexual intercourse. Some may be interested when they are older. Others may never be interested.

So sex is a lot of things . . . even feelings . . . and thoughts.

Sex is the desire to be very close to someone.

Sex is touching the sexual parts of the body.

Sex is intercourse.

Sex is making babies.

Sex is the label most babies are given at birth depending on which sexual parts they were born with—female parts, or male parts, or a mixture of male and female parts.

Sometimes people use the word *sexuality* to talk about sex. When people use the word *sexuality*, they are usually talking about everything in our daily lives that makes us sexual human beings—our gender, our sexual feelings, thoughts, and desires, as well as any sexual contact, from sexual touching to sexual intercourse.

5

Who We Are
Straight, Lesbian, Gay, Bisexual, Transgender, Queer, Questioning, +

S*traight, lesbian, gay,* and *bisexual* are words that have to do with sex because sex is also about sexual desire—the sexual feelings we may have toward another person. The words *sexual orientation* are words that have to do with sexual attraction.

Being sexually attracted to another person has to do with those sexual feelings one has toward that person. People do not choose their sexual orientation. Often it takes time for kids and for adults to figure out their sexual orientation. And different people have different sexual orientations.

A person who is straight is someone who is sexually attracted to people of another gender—someone who is not the same gender as they are. Heterosexual is another name for a straight person. *Heteros* is the ancient Greek word for *other.*

I like those Greek words.

I like pictures. I think a picture's worth a thousand words.

In a straight relationship, two people of different genders—a male and a female—are sexually attracted to, and may have loving feelings for or fall in love with, or may have a sexual relationship with each other.

A person who is gay is someone who is sexually attracted to people of the same sex or gender. Homosexual is another name for a gay person. *Homos* is the ancient Greek word for *same.* Now most people use the word *gay* instead of the word *homosexual.* In a gay relationship, two people of the same gender—a male and a male, or a female and a female—are attracted to, and may have loving feelings for or fall in love with, and may have a sexual relationship with each other.

A gay relationship between two females is also called a lesbian relationship. The word *lesbian* began to be used in the late nineteenth century. It refers to the time, about 600 BCE, when the great female poet Sappho lived on the Greek island of Lesbos. Sappho wrote about friendship and love between women.

The ancient Greeks thought that love between two men was the highest form of love. In the ancient Greek city-state of Sparta, in about 1000 BCE, it was hoped that if male warriors were in the same army

regiment as their lovers, they would fight harder in order to impress each other. The Spartan army was one of the most powerful and feared armies in ancient Greece.

A person who is bisexual is someone who is sexually attracted to people of a different gender and is also sexually attracted to people of the same gender. Someone who is bisexual is attracted to, may have a crush on, may have loving feelings for or fall in love with, and may have a sexual relationship with both males and females. *Bi* means *two* and is also the ancient Greek word for *two.* People often use the word *bi* for bisexual.

There have been gay, lesbian, and bisexual relationships all through history, even

before ancient Greece. How people feel and think about homosexuality and bisexuality has a lot to do with the culture and the times in which they live.

I love history. I love science too.

Don't brag.

Scientists do not completely understand or agree on why one person is straight, why another person is gay or lesbian, or why another person is bisexual. In fact, there may be more than one reason.

But most scientists believe that being lesbian, gay, straight, or bisexual is not something you choose—just as you cannot choose what skin color you were born with or the sex organs you were born with. They believe that a person is born with traits—with the biological makeup—and that those biological traits are what determine whether someone is a straight person, or a gay person, or a bisexual person.

Sometimes as kids are growing up, they become curious about other kids who are the same gender as they are or who are a different gender. They may even look at and even touch each other's bodies. This is a normal kind of exploring and does not necessarily have anything to do with whether someone is or will be straight, gay, lesbian, or bisexual.

Dreaming about or having a crush on a person of the same sex also does not necessarily mean that a person is or will be straight, gay, lesbian, or bisexual.

Whew! I'm glad it's okay to be curious about other bodies.

I myself am curious about celestial bodies.

Many people use the term LGBTQ+. These initials—*L* for *lesbian*, *G* for *gay*, *B* for *bisexual*, *T* for *transgender*, *Q* for *queer* or *questioning*, and + for *plus*— are ways of referring to people who are lesbian, gay, bisexual, transgender, or who refer to themselves as queer or questioning, or who may use other words to refer to themselves. *Queer* is a word that some people use to describe their gender and/or their sexuality. In the past, some used the word *queer* as an insult. Now many people are proud to identify themselves as queer. *Questioning* is a word that is used when people may question who they are sexually attracted to—someone of the same sex or gender as themselves, someone of a different sex or gender from themselves,

or both, or neither. The word *questioning* is also used when kids or adults question the feelings they have about their own gender.

Pansexual describes those who are attracted to people of all genders, not just to males or females.

Asexual is a word that is used to describe people who feel that they are not sexually attracted to anyone of any gender. The word *ace* is often used as a shorter way of saying asexual.

Gender is another word to describe who you are as a person. Gender can also be about the thoughts and feelings you have about who you are as a person.

There are many other things to know and many other words that have to do with gender. What is most important is to use words that are respectful when talking about gender. Chances are you have heard some of, but maybe not all of, these words. That's because over time some words that are used to describe gender do change, even though other words to describe gender stay the same. And soon, there may be new words that we use to describe gender.

Cisgender is a word that has to do with gender. *Cis* is the Latin word for the phrase "on the same side." A cisgender person is someone who feels or knows that the gender that was assigned to them at birth—female or male—was and still is their gender. The word *cis* is often used as a shorter way of saying the word *cisgender.* Cisgender people can be straight, or lesbian, or gay, or bisexual, or asexual.

Transgender is another word that has to do with gender.

Trans is the Latin word for *across* or the phrase *on another side.* A transgender person is someone whose gender identity is different from the gender that person was assigned at birth and who transitions from the gender assigned at birth to a different gender. Transgender people can be straight, or lesbian, or gay, or bisexual, or asexual.

This means that a person who was born with a male body, but feels, acts, and knows she is female and may ask to be

called a girl—or a person who was born with a female body, but feels, acts, and knows he is a male and may ask to be called a boy—is a transgender person. Some may feel this way all of the time and will feel this way throughout their lives. Others may feel this way for only a few months or a few years. And some may feel that sometimes they are one gender and other times they are a different gender.

Transgender people may change the way they dress or

their name to match the gender they believe they really are. They may also ask to be called "he" instead of "she" or "she" instead of "he." And some who feel that they are male some of the time and female at other times may ask to be called "they" or "them." It is always respectful and kind to ask people what name they want to be called and what pronouns—such as *they, she, he,* or *them*—they choose to use to refer to themselves and would like others to use when talking with or about them. It is also important to respect those who choose not to be identified or labeled by gender.

Oh-hhh . . . more words . . . to remember?

Say a word three times and you'll remember it.

Gender. Gender.

You only said it two times.

Said what?

Gender.

There are even more words that have to do with gender. And you may have noticed that other people may use words about gender that are different from the words you may have heard or may use.

The phrase *gender identity* describes the gender people identify with—the gender they feel and know they are.

Gender expression is about the many ways in which people express their gender to others, such as by the clothes one wears or by one's hairstyle.

Genderfluid describes those who feel they are not the same gender all of the time.

Pangender describes those who feel they are more than one gender. *Pan* is the ancient Greek word for *all.*

Binary, which means two, is a word that describes only two genders—female and male.

Non-binary is a word that can mean several things about a person's gender identity. It can mean that a person identifies as neither male nor female, or identifies as someone who is in between male and female, or may be another gender.

There are some who disapprove of people who are gay, lesbian, bisexual, transgender, or questioning

or call them offensive names, or tease, bully, or even hate them, or not want to be with them, only because a person is lesbian, gay, bisexual, transgender, or questioning. They may feel this way because they think LGBTQ+ people are different from them or that gay relationships are wrong. These people's views are based on fears or misinformation, not on facts. People are often afraid of people they know little or nothing about or who are different from them in some ways.

Some feel that transgender people should not have the right to use the bathroom at school or other public places or should not have the right to be on a sports team that aligns with the gender they feel or know they are. Taking away an LGBTQ+ person's rights only because of their gender identity or sexual orientation is more than disrespectful. Taking away or trying to take away one's rights can make a person feel sad, even very sad or angry. Yet, when this happens, there are people, including kids, who speak out in support of what is respectful and decent to do. Also, there are bathrooms in several schools and public

ALL GENDERS RESTROOM

places that have signs that say, ALL GENDERS or GENDER INCLUSIVE or GENDER NEUTRAL. That means that anyone, no matter what their gender, may use the bathroom. And there are schools that allow kids, no matter what their gender, to choose the team they want to be on.

Some people feel that LGBTQ+ people should not have the right to marry. Many other people feel and have always felt that LGBTQ+ people should have the right to marry. They now have that right. On June 16, 2015, the United States Supreme Court voted five to four to make it legal for people of the same sex to marry each other in all fifty states. The name of this Supreme Court decision is *Obergefell versus Hodges.* Until that date, same-sex marriage had been banned in most states. There are other countries that have also made it legal for people of the same sex to marry.

If a person has any questions, thoughts, or concerns about their sexual feelings or gender, talking to someone they know and trust—a parent, relative, therapist, doctor, nurse, teacher, or clergy person—can often be helpful.

No matter what some people may think, it's still important for every person to treat all people with respect. And it's important to know that people's daily lives—having fun, going to school, going to work, making a home, having friends, being in love, being single, being a partner, being married, raising children—are mostly the same whether someone is straight, gay, bisexual, transgender, queer, or questioning.

PART TWO

Our Bodies

6
The Human Body
All Kinds of Bodies

So many drawings and paintings and sculptures of the human body! Artists must love to draw the human body.

Artists love to draw the bee's body.

I haven't run across a painting of an insect.

Hold on. We haven't seen everything yet.

IT'S PERFECTLY NORMAL

7
Outside and Inside
Our Sex Organs

Everyone—babies, kids, teens, and grown-ups—are born with what many people call "sex organs." Many of our sex organs, but not all, are also our reproductive organs—the organs that can make a baby once our bodies have grown up and have become adult bodies.

Some of our sex organs are on the outside of our bodies. And some of our sex organs are inside our bodies. If they are on the outside, they are called outer sex organs. If they are on the inside, they are called inner sex organs.

The Female Sex Organs Outside

Most baby girls, girls, and women have what many people call "female sex organs"—sex organs that are on the outside of the body. These outer sex organs, the clitoris and the opening to the vagina, are hard to see because they are located between the legs.

The Vulva

The whole area of soft skin between a female's legs is called the vulva. The word *vulva* comes from the Latin word *volva*, which means *covering*. The vulva covers the clitoris, the opening to the vagina, the opening to the urethra, and the labia.

The Labia

The labia are two sets of soft folds of skin inside the vulva. They cover the inner parts of the vulva—the clitoris, the opening to the urethra, and the opening to the vagina. *Labia* is the Latin word for *lips.*

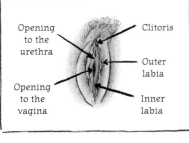

Vulva

The Clitoris

The clitoris is a small mound of skin about the size of a pea. When the clitoris is touched and rubbed, the clitoris and the whole body can feel good both outside and inside. It feels kind of tingly, kind of warm and nice. It feels sexy.

The Opening to the Urethra

The opening to the urethra is quite small. It is a tube through which urine—liquid waste—leaves the body. The urethra is not a reproductive organ.

> BODY FACT: Urine is liquid waste from the body, liquid left over from food and drink that is not used by the body. Urine is the only fluid that travels through a female's urethra.

The Opening to the Vagina

The opening to the vagina is a passageway between the uterus—a sex organ inside the female body—and the outside of the female body. The opening to the vagina is bigger than the opening to the urethra.

> BODY FACT: A thin piece of skin, called the hymen, covers part of the opening to the vagina. While a girl is growing, or is very active while exercising or playing a sport, or is using a tampon or a menstrual cup for the first time, or is having sexual intercourse for the first time, the hymen stretches and may tear and bleed a bit. And the opening to the vagina becomes somewhat larger. If some bleeding happens, it is normal. Usually, the bleeding does not continue.

The Anus

The anus is a small opening through which feces—solid waste—leave the body.

> BODY FACT: Solid waste is the solid material that is left over from food that is not used by the body. It leaves the female body in the same way that it leaves the male body. Solid waste is stored in the bowel before it leaves the body through the anus. The anus is not a reproductive organ.

For those who have female sex organs, in all, from front to back, there are three openings between their legs: the opening to the urethra, the opening to the vagina, and the anus. If they are curious about what these openings look like, holding a mirror between their legs is an easy way to find out what those parts look like.

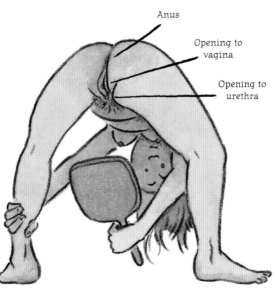

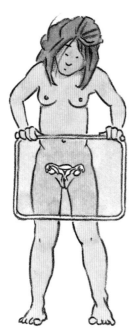

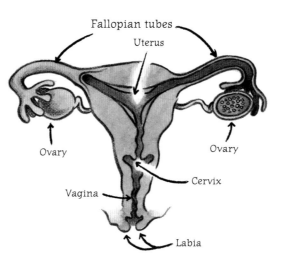

Fallopian tubes
Uterus
Ovary
Ovary
Cervix
Vagina
Labia

The Fallopian Tubes

The two fallopian tubes are passageways through which an egg travels on its way to the uterus. One end of each tube almost touches an ovary. The other end of each tube is connected to the uterus. Each tube is about three inches long and the width of a drinking straw.

Fallopian tubes

The Female Sex Organs Inside

Most baby girls, girls, and women also have female sex organs inside their bodies. If you could actually look inside a female body and see the inner sex organs, you would see two ovaries, two fallopian tubes, the uterus, and the vagina.

The Ovaries

The two ovaries — one on each side of the uterus — are about the size of large strawberries. The ovaries contain female sex cells, which are also called eggs or ova. A single egg is called an ovum.

BODY FACT: At birth, the ovaries already contain an astonishing number of egg cells—about one to two million. These egg cells are not grown up enough to produce babies until puberty begins. Female puberty—the time when the female body starts to grow into a young adult body—can begin anytime from about the age of eight or nine until fifteen. At puberty the ovaries have about three hundred to four hundred thousand egg cells. Egg cells are no longer able to produce babies after the female body is about age fifty.

Ovaries

The Uterus

The uterus is made of strong muscles and is hollow inside. It is about the size and shape of a small upside-down pear and is connected to both fallopian tubes and the inside end of the vagina.

BODY FACT: The uterus is the place in which a developing baby, called a fetus, grows, is fed, and is protected. A fetus grows in the uterus, which stretches as the fetus grows bigger, for about nine months until it is ready to be born. The uterus is sometimes called the womb.

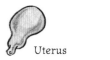

Uterus

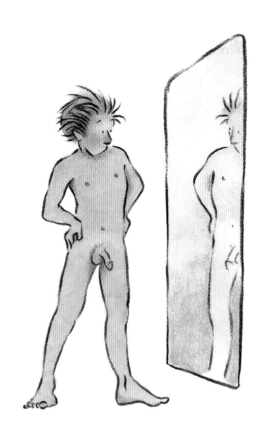

The Cervix

The cervix is a small opening located in the lower part of the uterus. It connects the uterus to the top of the vagina. This opening stretches wide when it's time for a baby to be born.

The Vagina

The vagina is the passageway from the uterus to the outside of the female body.

> BODY FACT: A baby travels through the vagina when it is ready to be born. The vagina is also the passageway through which a small amount of blood, other fluids, and tissue leave the uterus, about once a month. This small amount of normal bleeding begins during puberty and is called menstruation or "having a period." The vagina is also a place where the penis fits during sexual intercourse.

The Male Sex Organs Outside

Most baby boys, boys, and men have what many people call "male sex organs"—sex organs that are on the outside of the body. These outer sex organs, the penis and the scrotum—which contains the two testicles—are easy to see when the body is naked because they hang between the legs.

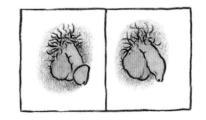

Circumcised   Uncircumcised
penis   penis

The Penis

The penis is made of soft, spongy tissue and blood vessels. Urine—liquid waste—leaves the male body through a small opening at the tip of the penis.

The end of the penis is called the glans. When the penis is touched and rubbed, the penis and the whole body can feel good both outside and inside—kind of tingly, kind of warm and nice. It feels sexy.

> BODY FACT: Generally, the penis is soft and hangs down over the scrotum. Sometimes, it becomes stiff and hard, and larger and longer, and stands out from the body. This is called an erection.

Anus

Scrotum

Penis

For those who have male sex organs, in all, from front to back, there are two openings between their legs: the small opening at the tip of the penis and the anus.

The Male Sex Organs Inside

If you could actually look inside a male body and see the inner sex organs, you would see two testicles and a series of tubes and glands that are connected to each other.

The Testicles

The two testicles are soft and squishy and are covered and protected by the scrotum. Usually one testicle hangs lower than the other. Before puberty each testicle is about the size of a marble. During puberty, each testicle grows to about the size of a walnut or a very small ball. That's why they are often called "nuts" or "balls."

> BODY FACT: Male sex cells, which are called sperm, are produced in the testicles. Unlike female sex cells, which exist at birth, male sex cells are not made until puberty begins. Male puberty—the time when the male body starts to grow into a young

At birth, some loose skin, called the foreskin, covers the end of the penis. Some parents choose to have their baby's foreskin removed a few days after birth, by a doctor or a specially trained religious person. This is called circumcision. Although a circumcised penis looks different from an uncircumcised penis, both work in the same way and equally well.

The Scrotum

The scrotum is the soft sac of wrinkly skin that covers, holds, and protects the two plum-shaped testicles.

The Anus

The anus is a small opening through which feces—solid waste—leave the body. The anus is not a reproductive organ.

> BODY FACT: Solid waste is the solid material that is left over from food that is not used by the body. It leaves the male body in the same way that it leaves the female body. Solid waste is stored in the bowel before it leaves the body through the anus.

Now we get to look inside again.

Oh, my. Do we have to?

adult body—can begin anytime from about the age of ten to about fifteen. At that time, the male body begins to produce sex cells, which are called sperm. The male body then continues to make sperm for many long years and into old age.

Testicles

The Epididymis

Each testicle is connected to its own small tubelike structure called the epididymis. Sperm travel through and "grow up" in the epididymis on their way to the vas deferens. Each epididymis is shaped like a set of headphones but is much smaller.

BODY FACT: Each epididymis is a tightly coiled thin tube, which, if stretched out, would be about twenty feet long.

Epididymis

The Vas Deferens

The two vas deferens are each about a foot and a half long. Each of these long, narrow, flexible, and fairly straight tubes starts at the epididymis and winds all the way to the

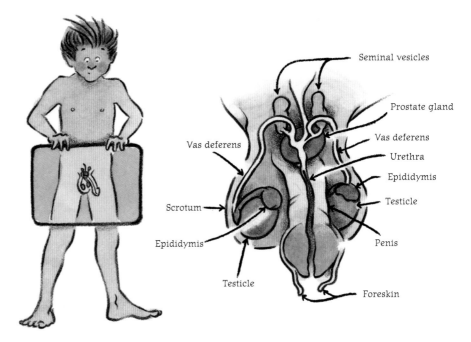

Seminal vesicles
Prostate gland
Vas deferens
Urethra
Epididymis
Testicle
Penis
Foreskin
Vas deferens
Scrotum
Epididymis
Testicle

urethra. The two vas deferens are about as flexible as strands of cooked spaghetti.

BODY FACT: Sperm cells travel from each testicle through the epididymis and the vas deferens.

Vas deferens

The Seminal Vesicles and the Prostate Gland

The two seminal vesicles and the prostate gland produce fluids that combine with the sperm to form a mixture called semen. *Semen* is the Latin word for *seed.* The sperm then travel along in the fluids to and through the urethra.

The Urethra

The urethra is a long, narrow tube that carries urine—liquid

waste—from the bladder, where it is stored, to the penis and out through the opening at its tip. It is also the passageway through which semen leaves the male body. The urethra is not a reproductive organ.

BODY FACT: Urine is liquid waste from the body, liquid left over from the food and drink that is not used by the body.

BODY FACT: Semen, the fluid that carries a male's sperm, leaves the male body in rapid spurts through the tip of the penis. This spurting is called ejaculation, and it occurs only after puberty has begun. Both semen and urine come out of the same opening at the tip of the penis. During ejaculation, muscles tighten and keep urine in the bladder so that urine does not leave the penis at the same time as semen.

8
Words
Talking About Bodies and Sex

Kids and grown-ups use all kinds of words for parts of the body and for sex. Some are scientific words. Some are unscientific—the common, everyday words that people use to talk about bodies and sex. Some of these words are nice, some are funny, and some are rude.

There are lots of silly-sounding words about sex and bodies—like "boobs" and "balls."

I much prefer the scientific words.

Everyday words are often called slang words. Rude and disrespectful words about sex and parts of the body are often called "dirty words." Jokes about bodies and sex are sometimes called "dirty jokes."

Some people think it's fun to use slang or dirty words and to joke about bodies and sex. Others feel embarrassed or uncomfortable when they hear these words. It's important to respect people's feelings about slang, dirty words, or dirty jokes, whatever those feelings may be.

Perhaps people feel uncomfortable talking about sex and bodies because we do not see our sexual body parts as much as we see our arms, legs, fingers, toes, ears, eyes, and noses. After all, our sexual body parts are usually covered by clothes.

Some people think it's wrong to think and talk or joke about bodies and sex. But many people think it can be comforting and helpful to talk or even joke about sex and bodies with someone you know and trust like a friend, a parent, an older brother or sister, or a cousin.

Did you ever notice that some grown-ups— not just kids— have a hard time talking about sex?

Yep! They twist around in their chairs and say "Well, uh ..." about a hundred times or laugh nervously.

The Joke

If you don't get the joke, you can always ask someone to explain it to you.

PART THREE

Puberty

9

Changes and Messages
Puberty and Hormones

Our bodies change from the moment we are born and keep on changing all through our lives. They change because everything that's alive grows and changes.

There is a time between the ages of eight or nine or ten or so to about age fourteen or fifteen or so when kids' bodies do more than just grow taller and bigger as they have done since birth. This is the time when kids' bodies start to grow into young adult bodies.

Puberty is one of the names given to this span of time. The word *puberty* comes from the

Latin word *pubertas,* which means *grown-up* or *adult.* When people use the word *puberty,* they are usually talking about all the physical changes that take place in kids' bodies during this time. Some kids' bodies start to change earlier. Some kids' bodies start to change later. Most of these changes make it physically possible for a person with a female body and a person with a male body to make a baby.

The other word that is used to describe the span of time between childhood and adulthood is *adolescence.* The word *adolescence* comes from the Latin word *adolescere,* which means *to grow up.* When people use the word *adolescence,* they are usually talking not only about the physical changes that take place during puberty, but also about all the new thoughts, feelings, relationships, and responsibilities kids have as they become young adults.

Even though the words *adolescence* and *puberty* have somewhat different meanings, people often use them interchangeably.

Puberty, or adolescence, is an in-between time—when kids are not quite children anymore, but are not quite adults yet—even though

they now have or almost have adult bodies. Some people call kids who are starting to go through puberty "tweens" or "tweenagers," because they are in between being a child and a teen.

I'm in-bee-tween. I hope bodies don't instantly pop into puberty!

I'd like that. You could get it all over with at once.

For most girls, puberty starts when they are nine or ten or eleven years old, but for some puberty may start earlier. For most boys, puberty starts a year or so later—when they are ten or eleven or twelve. For most kids, puberty takes place over a stretch of time—over a few years. This usually gives kids time to get used to their adult bodies.

The many changes that take place in our bodies during puberty are caused by hormones. Hormones are

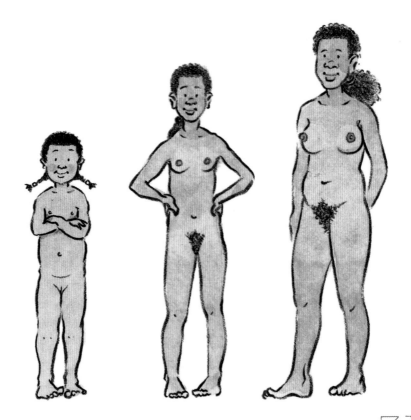

chemicals that are produced in many different places in our bodies. Hormones travel through the body's bloodstream from the place where they are made to other places in the body where they do their work.

The word *hormone* comes from the Greek word *hormon*, meaning *to set in motion*—to start something working. There are many kinds of hormones in our bodies.

During puberty, the brain begins to manufacture special hormones. These hormones send a message to the sex organs—the testicles or the ovaries—that tells them to start working—to start producing sex hormones.

The sex hormones in a male body then instruct the testicles to make sperm. The sex hormones in a female body then instruct the ovaries to send out an egg.

It is the sex hormones that cause the changes that make kids' bodies grow into adult bodies. Only then is it possible for humans to make babies. Once the sex hormones start working, puberty begins.

Some sex hormones cause changes to take place in and around kids' sex organs. Others cause changes to take place throughout their bodies.

Sex hormones can also affect kids' feelings and moods.

Many cultures, religions, communities, and families mark the beginning of puberty for their kids with a celebration or ceremony. They view puberty as a special part of growing up. Others choose to let their kids enter puberty without a celebration or ceremony. They view puberty simply as a regular and ordinary part of growing up.

I hope I don't have hormones floating around in me! I want my body to stay just the way it is now. I like it like this.

I'm ready for a change!

Let's throw a party to celebrate our growing up!

No way! My growing up is nobody's business but mine.

HELLO? OVARIES? BRAIN HERE. THIS IS YOUR PUBERTY WAKE-UP CALL! BIG CHANGES ARE COMING!

BRAIN

GREAT! WE'LL GET THOSE SEX HORMONES FLOWING RIGHT AWAY!

OVARY OVARY

HELLO? TESTICLES? BRAIN HERE. THIS IS YOUR PUBERTY WAKE-UP CALL! BIG CHANGES ARE COMING!

BRAIN

GREAT! WE'LL GET THOSE SEX HORMONES FLOWING RIGHT AWAY!

TESTICLES

10
The Travels of the Egg
Eggs and Puberty

"Start making female sex hormones!" is one of the messages the brain sends to the ovaries at puberty. And the ovaries do just that. They begin to produce the hormones estrogen and progesterone. Estrogen tells the eggs, which have been in the ovaries since birth, to grow up. Usually only one egg grows up at a time.

No one better start telling me to grow up!

I wish someone would.

When the eggs grow up, the ovaries do something they've never done before. About once a month, they release a single grown-up egg. An egg is about the size of a grain of sand.

Eggs are sex cells. The ovaries usually begin releasing eggs during puberty. Over the years, the ovaries will release about four hundred to five hundred eggs. The release of an

egg is called ovulation. The word *ovulation* comes from the Latin word *ovum*, meaning *egg*.

I do like those Latin words.

Sounds like Greek to me.

At about the same time every month, when an egg is released from one of the ovaries, it is swept by tiny finger-like projections into one of the fallopian tubes, where it begins its travel to the uterus.

The fallopian tube is the place where the egg can meet and unite with a sperm. Once an egg has united with a sperm, they become the beginning cell of a baby. The uniting of an egg cell and a sperm cell is called conception or fertilization.

The fertilized egg continues to travel through the fallopian tube and into the uterus, where the female sex hormone

progesterone has helped to create a soft lining that is ready to receive it. The fertilized egg then plants itself in the lining of the uterus. This soft, thick, cozy lining is made of extra blood vessels, tissue, and other fluids and is created so that the fertilized egg will have a healthy place to grow.

If the egg has been fertilized, it will usually plant itself in the uterus and stay there—and grow into a baby. However, most of the time, the egg is not fertilized. If the egg does not unite with a sperm within about twenty-four to thirty-six hours after leaving an ovary, it does not stay in the uterus and does not go on to develop into a baby.

Instead, the egg breaks down while it is in the uterus and mixes with some of the extra blood and fluid in the soft lining of the uterus. Since there is no fertilized egg starting to grow in the uterus, this soft lining is not needed and dissolves. It then passes out of the uterus, through the vagina, and out of the body

THE TRAVELS OF THE EGG: *Menstruation*

At puberty the brain tells the ovaries to produce estrogen, which tells the eggs to mature.

And then, about once a month, an egg leaves an ovary and pops into a fallopian tube,

where it waits before traveling to the uterus.

In the uterus, the egg and lining dissolve and leave. Next month . . .

in the form of a small amount of blood, other fluids, and tissue. The lining's monthly passing out of the uterus and the vagina is called menstruation. The word *menstruation* comes from the Latin word *mensis,* which means *month.*

The period of time from the beginning of one menstruation to the next is about a month long and is called the menstrual cycle. Menstruation usually starts after the ovaries have begun to release eggs. As soon as the ovaries have begun to release eggs, and if intercourse has occurred, a pregnancy can begin, but only if and when a united egg cell and sperm cell plants itself inside the lining of the uterus.

But some girls may begin to release eggs even before they start to menstruate. This means that it is possible, although quite rare, for a girl to become pregnant even before menstruation has begun. Girls usually start to menstruate at the age of eleven or twelve. But for some menstruation can start as early as age nine and for others it can start as late as age fifteen, and both are perfectly normal.

The very first time most girls menstruate, they may worry that a large amount of blood will suddenly flow out. In fact, the blood usually comes out slowly. Only a few tablespoonfuls to about half a cup of blood and tissue dribble out during each menstruation. But the amount can be more or less, and that's also perfectly normal.

This dribbling continues over a period of a few days. That's why people call menstruation a menstrual period or "having your period." Others may call menstruation "my friend," "my cycle," or "that time of the month," or may have different names or their own names for menstruation. No matter what people call it, menstruation is a healthy occurrence.

A period usually lasts about three to eight days. When menstruation starts, periods often come irregularly—sometimes a few weeks apart, sometimes many weeks apart. It can often take up to one or two years for a girl's period to occur on a regular schedule—about once a month. For some, their periods never become very regular. If that happens, it's a good idea to check with a nurse or a doctor—just to make sure their periods are normal.

Most people who are menstruating usually continue their regular activities during menstruation. They bathe, shower, swim, play sports, dance, and do whatever they normally like to do. Some do get cramps— usually slight, tight pains around the area of the uterus— before and during their periods. Most cramps are normal. But if a person's cramps hurt a lot during a period, or if there is heavy bleeding during a period that may make it hard to go to school, or cause one to stay home and not go to school or not go out with friends, it's a good idea to see your doctor or nurse, who may be able to help you feel better.

When traveling, playing sports vigorously, losing or gaining a lot of weight, or becoming upset or ill, periods can become irregular for a while. When a person becomes pregnant, periods stop occurring until after the baby is born.

When the female body is about fifty years old, it starts to make fewer sex hormones. As a result, the ovaries stop releasing eggs, and that's when the female body stops menstruating. This period of time is called menopause—the pausing and stopping of menstruation. When a person stops having menstrual periods, that person is no longer able to become pregnant.

During a menstrual period, pads or tampons are used to

absorb the menstrual flow—the blood—that passes out of the vagina so it will not leak on underpants or other clothes. Some use a menstrual cup, which can collect the menstrual blood as it flows out of the vagina. A person can use whichever method feels most comfortable.

Pads are also called sanitary napkins. *Sanitary* means *clean.*

Pads and tampons are made of a clean, soft, cottonlike material and absorb the menstrual flow. Pads fit on the inside of a pair of underpants, just outside the opening to the vagina. They have a special tape on them that sticks onto underpants to keep the pad in place.

Tampons fit inside the vagina. A tampon cannot move into the uterus because the cervix is too small an opening for a tampon to pass through.

Menstrual cups also fit inside the vagina. They are shaped like a small bell and are made of rubber, soft plastic, or silicone. Some cups can be reused during a period. But the blood collected in the cup needs to be emptied into a toilet whenever it's full, and then washed and placed back into the vagina. Menstrual cups can be thrown away after using only one time

and replaced with a new cup, or the same cup can be used during a period and thrown away after each period.

Many girls wonder when they might get their first period. If a girl's birth mother started menstruating early, there's a good chance the daughter may start early too. If a girl's birth mother started later, there's a good chance that the daughter may start later.

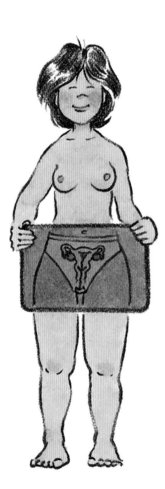

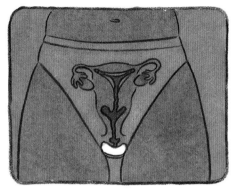

Where a Pad Fits

Pads

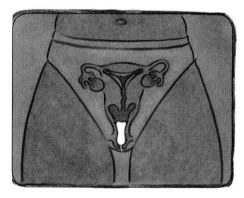

Where a Tampon Fits

Tampons

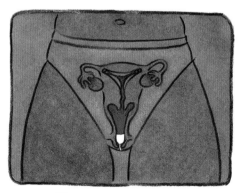

Where a Menstrual Cup Fits

Menstrual Cup

Talking to someone about menstruation—one's mother or grandmother or aunt, or an older friend or cousin—can be helpful. One can find out many useful things from someone who is already menstruating or has already stopped menstruating, such as what it feels like to menstruate, what needs to be done to get ready for one's first period, where to get pads or tampons or menstrual cups, and how to use them. This kind of information can help to prepare for a first period—whether it starts at home or when out with friends or in school. It's also a good idea to carry a pad or tampon in a purse or backpack in case a first period begins while away from home.

Pad? All I need is a launchpad!

Not me. I soar straight up to the sky!

No matter how well prepared a person is, a first period usually comes as somewhat of a surprise. For some, it may feel quite exciting; for others, a bit scary. But no matter how someone feels, starting to menstruate is a perfectly normal and natural part of growing up. Many kids feel that starting to menstruate is one of the biggest changes of puberty.

Once a person begins to menstruate and release sex cells, if just one egg unites with one sperm during sexual intercourse, a pregnancy can begin once the united cell plants itself inside the uterus. This is when the united cell can begin to develop into a fetus. The moment of birth is when the fetus becomes a baby.

So in the uterus, it's a fetus.

Congrats! You got it right!

And at birth, it's an adorable, sweet, little, brand-new, cutie-pie baby.

Congrats again! You got it right again!

11

The Travels of the Sperm
Sperm and Puberty

"Start making the male sex hormone testosterone!" is one of the messages the brain sends to the testicles at puberty. And the testicles do just that. They begin to produce the testosterone, which causes the body to grow and change in many new ways.

One of the most important things testosterone does is instruct the testicles to begin to make sperm—something the testicles have never done before.

Seems like puberty's a busy time.

Busy as a bee!

Sperm are sex cells. Unlike egg cells, which are already in the ovaries before birth, the testicles do not start making sex cells until they reach puberty. Starting at puberty, however, the testicles make a phenomenal number of sperm—about one hundred million to three hundred million sperm per day. That's anywhere from about one thousand to three thousand sperm every second.

The scrotum protects the testicles by keeping them at the right temperature to make sperm, not too cold and not too hot, just a few degrees below the body's temperature. If it is too cold, the scrotum pulls up the testicles closer to the body to keep them warm enough to make sperm. When swimming in cold water, a boy or man can often feel the scrotum tighten as it pulls the testicles up. If it is too hot, the scrotum hangs down loosely, away from the body, again keeping the testicles at just the right temperature to make sperm.

After sperm are produced, the sperm from the right testicle travel through the right epididymis, and the sperm from the left testicle travel through the left epididymis. As they travel, the sperm grow up enough to be able to fertilize—to unite with—an egg.

Sperm travel through the vas deferens and pass by the seminal vesicles. As sperm pass by, they mix with fluid from the seminal vesicles and the prostate gland.

The mixture of sperm and fluid is now called semen. Semen is sticky, cloudy, and whitish. Chemicals in it keep the sperm healthy as they travel into the urethra, through it, and out the tip of the penis. Sperm leave the body when a penis ejaculates semen. To *ejaculate* means *to suddenly release* or *to let go*. When ejaculation occurs, the penis is usually erect.

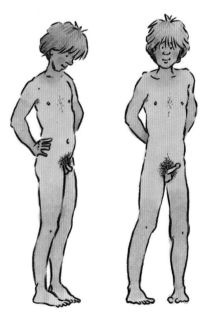

THE TRAVELS OF THE SPERM: *Ejaculation*

At puberty the brain tells the testicles to produce testosterone and sperm.

Sperm travel to the epididymis, where they mature and travel

through the vas deferens, past the seminal vesicles and prostate gland,

through the urethra, and are spurted out the tip of the penis.

Here's what happens inside the penis during an erection: When the penis is not erect, blood trickles in and out of the penis continuously. During an erection, the muscles that allow blood to flow in and out of a penis open wide and allow more blood to be pumped in, while other muscles tighten and keep the extra amount of blood from leaving the penis. This causes the spongy tissue inside the penis to fill up, which in turn makes the penis become stiff, erect, and stand out from the body. This filling up is called an erection.

When the erection is over, the muscles relax and allow the blood to flow back out of the penis and into the body again. And the penis becomes soft again.

Erections can happen when the penis is touched and rubbed, or when a boy or man is having pleasurable thoughts or seeing someone who makes them feel happy, excited, sexy, or nervous. Erections can also happen when watching a movie or TV show or video or reading or seeing something online that feels exciting, when someone attractive walks by, or while having a pleasurable dream.

Many boys and men often have erections when they wake

up. If the bladder—the place where urine is stored in the body—is full, the full bladder excites some nerves at the base of the penis, which causes more blood to flow into the penis. This kind of erection has little to do with sexy thoughts and feelings.

Erections usually happen before and during sexual intercourse. An erection makes it possible for the penis to enter the vagina. Sometimes erections happen for no apparent reason, even when one doesn't want to have them.

Some people call an erection a "hard-on" or "boner" even though there are no bones in the penis. Erections can last a few seconds, or a few minutes, or sometimes a half-hour or

more. Male fetuses inside the uterus can have erections. Male babies can also have erections. Males can have erections when they are asleep. And males can continue to have erections into old age.

Here's what happens inside the body during an ejaculation: Muscles in each epididymis, in each vas deferens, and in the seminal vesicles, along with muscles around the prostate gland, tighten and push the semen into the urethra. The semen, which contains sperm, travels through the urethra and spurts out through the tip of the penis. This spurting out of semen—ejaculation—causes a feeling of excitement called an orgasm.

During ejaculation, muscles tighten so that urine does not leave the penis at the same time as semen. After ejaculation, the penis becomes soft again and is no longer erect.

There are usually about two to five hundred million sperm spurted out in a single ejaculation—about a teaspoonful of semen. But an erection can happen without ejaculating any semen. When this happens, the blood leaves the penis slowly and returns to the body's bloodstream, the erection slowly goes away, and the penis becomes soft again and hangs down as usual. It is possible, although this does not happen often, to ejaculate without having an erection.

Most boys start to be able to ejaculate during puberty and continue into old age. Ejaculation usually occurs during sexual intercourse. It can also occur during other kinds of sexual touching and excitement and even during sleep.

Most boys usually start having "wet dreams" at puberty. Wet dreams happen when a pleasurable, exciting, or sexy dream causes the penis to ejaculate some semen. When one wakes up, their pajamas or sheets may be wet and sticky from the ejaculated semen.

The scientific term for a wet dream is *nocturnal emission. Nocturnal* means *occurring at night. Emission* means *a release, a letting go.* Wet dreams are usual and normal events for boys. A boy's first ejaculation often happens during a dream. Many kids feel that starting to ejaculate is one of the biggest changes of puberty.

Once the body has begun to produce sperm, if just one sperm unites with an egg during sexual intercourse, a pregnancy can begin once the united cell plants itself inside the lining of the female's uterus. This is when the united cell can begin to develop into a fetus. At birth is when the fetus becomes a baby.

12
Not All at Once!
Growing and Changing Bodies

During puberty, sex hormones cause kids to grow and change in even more ways.

All these changes do not take place at once. Most happen slowly over a few years' time; a few happen quickly. And they often, although not always, take place in a somewhat specific order.

Puberty Changes: The Female Body

Most girls experience these changes in puberty:

• Ovaries gradually grow larger.

• Body sweats more.

• Skin and hair become more oily.

• Body has a sudden growth spurt.

• Body gains some weight and grows taller.

• Arms and legs grow longer.

• Hands and feet grow bigger.

• Bones in the face grow larger and longer, and the face looks less childlike.

• Soft, darkish hair grows around the vulva and later becomes curly, thick, and coarse.

• A tiny bit of sticky whitish fluid may come out of the vagina.

> PUBERTY FACT: The whitish fluid that may flow out of the vagina is normal and helps keep it clean and healthy.

• Hips grow wider. Body begins to look more curvy.

> PUBERTY FACT: Hips grow wider, so that if and when one decides to have a baby, the baby will have enough room to leave the uterus when it is ready to be born.

• Hair grows under the arms.

• Breasts and nipples gradually grow larger and fuller.

> PUBERTY FACT: Breasts grow larger and fuller to prepare the body to make milk to nurse one's baby if and when a baby is born.

• Nipples may become a darker color.

• Menstruation can begin.

> PUBERTY FACT: Once the ovaries have grown larger, they start to release grown-up eggs, and menstruation begins. Once menstruation starts, and if a female and a male have intercourse, and an egg and sperm unite, and that united cell plants itself in the female's uterus, that's when a pregnancy can begin.

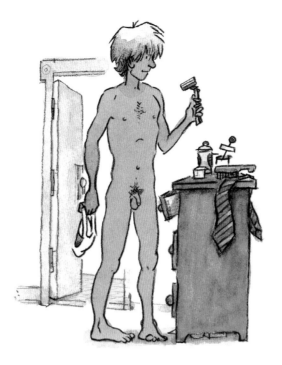

Puberty Changes: The Male Body

Most boys experience these changes in puberty:

- Testicles gradually grow larger and fuller.
- Penis gradually grows larger and longer.
- Body sweats more.
- Skin and hair become more oily.
- Body has a sudden growth spurt.
- Body gains weight and grows taller.
- Arms and legs grow longer.
- Hands and feet grow larger.
- Bones in the face grow, and the face looks less childlike.
- Soft, darkish hair grows around the base of the penis and later becomes curly, thick, and coarse.

- Hair grows under the arms.
- Shoulders and chest grow bigger.
- Bigger muscles develop.
- Scrotum turns a darker color.
- Hair grows on the face, first the mustache, then the beard and sideburns.
- Hair grows on the chest.

PUBERTY FACT: Sometimes the area around the nipples may feel sore and may even swell. This is caused by the hormones that are released during puberty. The soreness and swelling go away after a few months.

- The larynx, or as it is commonly called, the voice box, grows bigger.
- The voice cracks and then becomes deeper.

- The Adam's apple may begin to show more.

PUBERTY FACT: When most boys' voices begin to change, one second their voices can sound high, one second low, and the next high again, causing a cracking-squeaky sound. But after a while, a boy's voice begins to sound deeper and lower, because the larynx and vocal cords have grown. As the larynx grows bigger, it may push the Adam's apple forward, causing it to show more.

- Sperm begin to be produced.
- Ejaculations—including wet dreams—begin to occur.

PUBERTY FACT: Once a male body can make sperm, and if a female's ovaries have started to release eggs, and if the male and the female have intercourse, and their sperm and egg unite and plants itself inside the uterus, that's when a pregnancy can begin.

At this age, kids' bodies change more dramatically and rapidly than at any other time in their lives—except for the very first year of life.

I'd just as soon go back in time.

I'm ready to move on.

13
More Changes!
Taking Care of Your Body

Many of the physical changes that take place during puberty cause kids' bodies to work in many new ways. This means that kids have to learn some new ways to take care of their bodies.

Oh good! More changes!

Give me a break.

Kids grow more hair during puberty. They grow hair under their arms. For some kids, hair that is on their arms and legs grows thicker and longer.

Hair called pubic hair grows around the vulva and around the base of the penis—directly in front of a bone called the pubic bone.

During puberty, hair grows on kids' faces, chests, arms, and legs. The amount of hair that grows is different for different kids. Some kids grow hardly any hair. Some grow some hair. Some grow a lot of hair. Whatever amount one grows is perfectly normal.

Some kids start shaving during puberty. For most kids, shaving is a choice. Some choose to shave the hair that grows under their arms and on their legs, and some don't. Some choose to shave their beards and mustaches, and some don't. However, some religious groups require that their boys and men not use a razor or scissors to cut their hair.

During puberty, kids' sweat glands produce more sweat than before. They start to sweat under their arms and develop a new kind of body odor, sometimes from under their arms, sometimes from their feet, and sometimes from all over their bodies.

That's one of the reasons kids going through puberty take a lot of baths or showers and wash their bodies and hair a lot. This new kind of sweating is often one of the first signs that puberty is starting. Washing with soap and using a deodorant can help get rid of most strong body odors.

Some kids sweat a lot. Some kids sweat a little. It is likely that you will sweat about the

same amount as one of your parents, whose sperm and egg joined together to make you, did while they were going through puberty.

Some kids' hair becomes oily during puberty. Often some oiliness also begins to appear on kids' noses and foreheads.

During puberty, most kids develop pimples on their faces—mostly on their noses

and foreheads. Sometimes, kids develop pimples on their backs and chests. Many kids call pimples "zits."

Although careful washing with soap and water is a good way to care for the skin, sometimes it is not enough. Creams and medicines can help control pimples. Some creams and medicines can be purchased at a drugstore without a doctor's written prescription; others need to be prescribed by a doctor and then purchased from a pharmacist or online.

Though it's true no one likes having pimples, having them is perfectly normal. Kids develop pimples and/or oily hair and sweat more during puberty because their oil and sweat glands are more active than ever before.

Since puberty is the time when many girls' breasts begin

to grow bigger, this is often the time they start, if they choose, to wear bras. *Bra* is short for the word *brassiere*. A girl often goes with a family member, or a good friend, to buy a first bra.

It is not necessary to wear a bra to keep breasts healthy. Those who wear bras do so because they feel more comfortable wearing them. Some wear a bra only when they are exercising or playing a sport. Others wear one all the time, except when sleeping. And some wear one when sleeping. Still others never wear a bra at all. No matter what size breasts someone has, it's important to buy a bra that fits correctly and is comfortable. Bras are made with different size cups in order to support various breast sizes.

Many boys and men wear jockstraps when playing sports. A jockstrap fits over the testicles and penis, keeping them in place and protecting them from bruises or injuries. When playing some contact sports such as soccer, football, hockey, baseball, or lacrosse, a plastic cup, called an athletic cup, can be slipped into the front of the jockstrap to provide even more protection for the testicles and penis. Athletic cups also come in various sizes.

Small and medium and large cups...

And teacups...

And A and B and C and D cups and...

All these are giving me the hiccups!

But if the testicles feel tender or painful, it's a good idea to see a doctor or nurse to help you feel better.

Kids' bodies change in so many ways during puberty that taking care of them can at times be a chore. However, eating healthy foods, exercising and keeping fit, keeping clean, and getting enough sleep can help kids feel healthy and good about all the growing and changing that goes on.

14
Back and Forth, Up and Down
New and Changing Feelings

The many changes that take place in kids' bodies during puberty are often accompanied by new and strong feelings about how their bodies look, feel, and act—and by new and strong feelings about growing up and sex.

Many kids find these changes exciting and feel great about their bodies. And just as many find these changes overwhelming and feel shy or embarrassed about their changing bodies. Most kids, at one time or another during puberty, feel confused or uncomfortable, and some may even feel worried or scared by these big and sometimes rapid changes.

Kids often wonder about the size of individual body parts. The truth is—whether small, medium, or large—the size of a person's body parts has nothing to do with how well they work.

It is also true that different kids' bodies develop in different ways. Some girls develop small breasts, others develop medium-size breasts, and still others develop large breasts. Some boys develop small penises, others develop medium-size penises, and still others develop large penises. Breasts and penises come in all sorts of sizes.

The size of most girls' breasts—small or medium or large—may resemble their mother's, or grandmother's, or another female relative's breasts. The amount of body hair most boys develop—a small amount or a regular amount or a lot of hair—may resemble the amount of body hair their father, or grandfather, or another male relative has developed. The size of any part of a person's body is mostly inherited from a person's family.

The age when kids begin puberty is often the same as it was for a close family member of the same sex. You might want to ask your parent or other family members what puberty was like for them and when they began to go through it. You might find some clues about how you may develop.

Enough already about these changes!

What's the big deal? You'll still have the same body.

But I bet at times it won't feel like the same body.

It's hard to be an early bloomer … or a late bloomer.

I just need the flowers to bloom. I don't care when they bloom.

Kids often wonder whether it matters if their bodies go through puberty slow or fast, early or late, or first or last. When your body changes, or how fast or slowly your body changes, has nothing to do with how your body will look and perform.

Even so, among one's friends or in one's class, it can be hard to be the first or last

who menstruates, or the first or last whose voice changes; or the first or last to wear a bra, or the first or last to shave; or to be the shortest kid one year and the tallest the next year.

Unfortunately, kids tease other kids about the ways their bodies look and grow during puberty. A kid's arms, hands, legs, and feet may grow longer and bigger before the rest of their body catches up. Or a kid may develop a large pimple on the forehead just before going to a party. Or a kid's voice may crack right in the middle of a sentence. Often these are the kinds of things kids are teased about as they go through puberty.

Many kids worry about their friendships during

puberty—probably because puberty is a time when some kids start to have loving relationships with other kids. One of your friends, even your best friend, may begin to be interested in and sexually attracted to other kids, whereas you are not the least bit interested. One of your friends may start to have a partner and spend a lot time with that person. Or you may have a partner when your best friend doesn't.

Sometimes kids feel upset or jealous when a friend has a partner and starts spending a lot of time with that person. Although many old friendships stay strong during puberty, some friendships change. Having a loving relationship and having a partner are other things kids are teased about during puberty.

With all the different things that happen to their bodies during puberty, it's no wonder kids have so many different feelings. Kids can often feel moody or crabby or even teary and cry more than usual. And your moods can change quickly. Or you may be laughing one moment and feel like crying the next moment.

These different feelings often swing back and forth and up and down, like a yo-yo. The increased activity of the sex hormones is one of many factors that causes kids to have mood swings as well as new and strong feelings during puberty.

As kids' bodies change into grown-up bodies, kids are not always sure that they are ready to be grown-up. Sometimes they want to be treated as kids. Other times they want to be treated as adults. Some may feel uncomfortable or upset about the changes that are happening to their bodies and about the many different feelings they may be having during puberty. Others may feel proud and excited.

Changing from a kid to an adult has its difficult moments. But sooner or later, most kids get used to, become comfortable with, and feel good about their grown-up bodies.

The sooner I change the better.

Later is better for me.

15
Perfectly Normal
Masturbation

During puberty, when the sex hormones cause kids' sex organs to become more active, many kids begin to have even more pleasurable and excited feelings about their own bodies than they have ever had before. They may also be more attracted to and interested in other people's bodies.

These feelings are often called sexual feelings or "feeling sexy." Even though they are hard to describe, they are normal feelings. They happen at different times and in different ways for different kids.

Kids, teenagers, and grown-ups too experience sexy feelings when they masturbate. Masturbation is touching or rubbing any of your body's sex organs for pleasure—because it feels good. One everyday term people young and old often use for masturbating is "playing with yourself."

Some people think that masturbation is wrong or harmful. And some religions call masturbation a sin. But masturbating cannot hurt you. And it does not result in pregnancy or in getting or passing on infections that are spread through sexual contact.

Many people masturbate. Many don't. Whether you masturbate or not is your choice. Masturbating is perfectly normal.

When people masturbate, they usually rub their sex organs with their hands or with something soft, like a pillow.

Girls often rub their clitoris; boys often rub their penis. Both the clitoris and the penis are sensitive to touch.

Mas-tur-bat-ing. I've heard about that.

Just another big word. That's all it is.

A person may have a warm, good, tingly, exciting feeling all through their body while masturbating. This feeling can become more and more intense until it reaches a peak or climax. At that moment, a male may ejaculate; a female may feel strong, exciting sensations just in the area around the vulva or throughout the body. A female may also feel some wetness in the vagina.

When this happens, this is called having an orgasm. Some people call it "coming." After having an orgasm, a person usually feels quite content and relaxed.

Often, but not always, people have orgasms when they masturbate or when they have sexual intercourse. Kids may also have orgasms during a dream. Some may have orgasms for no particular reason at all. People may have orgasms at some times and not at other times. Not everyone has orgasms.

Often when people masturbate, they daydream about someone or something happy or pleasurable or sexy. Some people become sexually excited without masturbating, just by looking at sexy pictures or by dreaming about or having

fantasies about something pleasurable.

People of all ages masturbate—babies, kids, teenagers, grown-ups, and the elderly. Girls and boys often start to masturbate at puberty, but many start before.

I've heard enough about sex for now.

Not me.

PART FOUR

Families and Babies

16
All Sorts of Families
Taking Care of Babies and Kids

Babies and children grow up in all sorts of families. Kids live in families whose parents live together, or whose parents live apart. Kids live in families who have only one parent, or in families whose parent or parents have adopted them. There are kids who live with one of their parents and that parent's partner some of the time and also live with their other parent and that parent's partner some of the time. Kids live in families with a parent and a stepparent, or with an aunt, an uncle, or a grandparent, or other relative. Kids live in families who have straight, lesbian, gay, or transgender parents, or who have foster parents.

Grandparents and cousins and uncles and aunts are also part of a person's family. And

some people feel that their good friends are part of their families too. Most kids are loved and taken care of by family members and family friends.

My family's left the nest—flown the coop.

My family sticks together—around the hive.

Bringing a baby into this world is an important and exciting event. Becoming a parent is one of the biggest changes that can happen to a person. It brings with it all sorts of new and different responsibilities.

These responsibilities include taking good care of oneself as well as of one's baby and family. That's why the decision about when to start a family is so important. Although it is physically possible for most girls and most boys to make a baby, once most girls have begun to menstruate (and in rare instances even before) and most boys have begun to produce sperm, it makes good sense for people to wait until they are ready and old enough to take on such big responsibilities.

Having a baby when a person is too young can be difficult. There are lots of reasons for this. Babies of kids and young teenagers are often born weighing too little even after a full nine months in the

uterus. Babies who weigh too little are more likely to have health problems at birth and as they grow up.

Babies are pretty cute. Something to love—so soft and cuddly.

But you don't have to take care of one all day long, all night long, day in, day out, feed the baby, give it a bath, watch it, play with it, get it dressed and undressed, change its diaper . . .

I get the picture.

Parents often find it hard to care for a baby, especially if they are still kids or young teenagers. Kids or young

costs a lot of money to pay someone to take care of a baby while they go to school or work.

Babies are very special and mothers and fathers love their babies a lot, whether a parent is younger or older or in between. Most often, but not always, it's easier and healthier for kids and teenagers to wait until they are older to have a baby. It gives the baby and the parents a better chance to have a healthy start together. However, if parents are quite young when they have a baby, some are still able to take good care of their baby. Often their parents or another family member or friend helps them raise a healthy baby.

teenagers who have a baby often lose the freedom to do what they want to do. It's hard to go out with friends or to get schoolwork done when a baby is around. Babies need a lot of attention, day in, day out, every day, every night.

Teenagers who have babies often drop out of school because they need to work. It costs a lot of money to buy food, clothes, toys, and medicine for a baby. It's often hard for teenagers to get a job to pay for these things. And it

17
Instructions — Information
The Cell: Genes and Chromosomes

All living creatures start out as a single cell. When two sex cells—an egg and a sperm—unite into a single cell, they carry all the information required to make a new baby—a new human being. This information is stored in more than one hundred thousand genes in the center of the cell.

Some scientists describe genes as little packages of instructions. Your genes helped to decide all sorts of things about you—the color of your eyes, the shape of your ears, the type and color of your hair, the color of your skin, and whether you are born with female body parts or male body parts or with a mixture of male and female body parts.

Or the color of your blue jeans.

Not those kinds of jeans!

Your genes were passed on to you from two parents whose egg cell and sperm cell joined together to make you. These parents are called your birth or biological parents. And their genes from their parents and through them from earlier generations on both sides of your family can also be passed on to you. If you were adopted, your genes were also passed on to you by your birth or biological parents and through them to you from earlier generations on both sides of your family. If you become a parent and are the birth parent of a child, many of your genes will also be passed on to your child and grandchildren from you and from earlier generations of your family.

Genes are made of DNA— a short name for a chemical called deoxyribonucleic acid. Genes are carried on long, threadlike strings of DNA called chromosomes. A gene is a tiny part of a chromosome. A chromosome is the part of each cell that carries a person's

genes. You might picture a chromosome as a string of beads, with each bead as a gene.

A chromosome

Cells in the human body usually have forty-six chromosomes. But each egg cell and each sperm cell carries only twenty-three chromosomes. If an egg and a sperm unite, the combined single cell has a grand total of forty-six chromosomes.

So 23 chromosomes plus 23 chromosomes IS 46 chromosomes!

But that does NOT make you a math genius!

That means half your chromosomes, as well as half your DNA, comes from the person whose egg cell joined together with a sperm cell to make you and the other half comes from the person whose sperm cell joined together with that egg cell to make you. You received a combination of genes from both of them. While you are not an exact copy of either one of your birth parents, you probably do resemble each of them in some ways, but not in all ways.

I'm a combination of my mom and my dad. I've got my father's wings and my mother's eyes.

I've got my mother's wings and my father's feet.

If two eggs leave the ovaries at the same time, and if each egg is fertilized by a separate sperm, fraternal, or nonidentical, twins begin. Since fraternal twins do not have the same genes, they do not look exactly like each other and can be the same sex or another sex.

2 eggs + 2 sperm   Fraternal twins

Identical twins begin if a single egg splits into two after it has been fertilized. Since identical twins have the same genes, they are always the same sex and look almost exactly like each other.

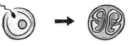

1 egg + 1 sperm   Identical twins

When two or more babies are born at the same birth—twins, triplets, and so on—it is called a multiple birth.

Unless you are an identical twin, you are not an exact genetic copy of your brother or sister, because a different sperm and egg united to form every new baby. Each sperm and each egg carries a different combination of genes. That's why you can look somewhat different or very different from your sister or brother.

Scientists have discovered that a person's sex organs—whether a person is born with female body parts, or male body parts, or a mixture of male and female body parts—are determined the moment an egg cell and a sperm cell unite and become one cell.

Among the twenty-three chromosomes that are in each egg cell and in each sperm cell is one sex chromosome. There are two kinds of sex chromosomes—an X chromosome and a Y chromosome. All eggs carry an X chromosome and all sperm carry either an X or a Y chromosome.

I've read that some honeybees have 16 chromosomes. And some have 32 chromosomes. That's sweet!

Birds have 80 chromosomes! That's cool!

When an egg is fertilized by a sperm—and if that sperm's Y chromosome unites with that egg's X chromosome—that united single cell will then carry a combined XY chromosome. And that united cell will usually develop into a person who will be born with male body parts.

When an egg is fertilized by a sperm—and if that sperm's X chromosome unites with that egg's X chromosome—that united single cell will then carry a combined XX chromosome. And that united cell will usually develop into a person who will be born with female body parts.

Sometimes, when an egg is fertilized by a sperm, the ways in which the chromosomes unite in that united single cell may mean that the united cell will develop into a person who is born with a mixture of female and male body parts. A mixture of female and male body parts is often called "intersex."

Whether you were born male or female was determined by which chromosome—an X or a Y—was in the sperm that fertilized the egg that created you.

Whether you were born intersex was also determined by the ways these chromosomes united at the moment the sperm and egg that made you became one cell.

The genes inside your body carry lots of information about you and determine many things—but not everything—about you.

Where you are brought up and how you are brought up, including the kind of food you eat and the kind of exercise you get, as well as the people who are around you and the events that occur as you grow up, also help to shape many things about you. That's why no two people in the world—even identical twins—are exactly alike. Each of us is unique.

I'm one of a kind.

Thank goodness for that.

18
A Kind of Sharing
Cuddling, Kissing, Touching, and Sexual Intercourse

Sexual intercourse, or as it is often called, "making love," is a kind of sharing between two people—between a female and a male, or between two females, or between two males.

Touching, caressing, kissing, and hugging—often called "making out"—are other kinds of sharing that can make two people feel very close and loving and excited about each other. People can and do become sexually excited without having sexual intercourse.

When two people feel loving and excited about each other, but also feel they are too young to have sexual intercourse, do not know each other well enough, or do not want to have sexual intercourse for any other reason, they may decide just to talk with each other, or hold hands, or cuddle, or dance, or kiss, or make out.

Deciding to wait to have sexual intercourse until one is older or feels more responsible is called postponement. Deciding not to have sexual intercourse is called abstinence.

Sharing between two people who care about each other always means having respect for each other's feelings and wishes. That's why before having any kind of sexual activity with each other, including sexual intercourse, both people need to agree whether or not to do so. If they agree, this is called "giving consent." Giving consent means that both people must say "yes" to each other. And consent always includes respecting and agreeing with each other's right to say "No!" to any kind of sexual activity—from touching

to sexual intercourse—at any time and for any reason.

Sexual intercourse usually begins with two people touching, caressing, kissing, and hugging each other.

After a bit, a person's vagina becomes moist and slippery, and the clitoris becomes hard. After a bit, a person's penis becomes erect, stiff, and larger. Sometimes a bit of clear fluid that may contain a few sperm comes out of the tip of the penis and makes it wet. This is usually when two people begin to feel excited about each other.

But in fact, there are different kinds of sexual intercourse—vaginal intercourse, oral intercourse, and anal intercourse.

When a person with a female body and a person with a male body are having vaginal intercourse, the erect penis goes into and inside the vagina, which stretches in a way that fits around the penis. The wetness from the vagina makes it easier for the penis to go into the vagina.

Vaginal intercourse is also called vaginal sex. As the two people move back and forth in rhythm, the movement of the penis inside the vagina soon feels very good. They may hug and kiss and touch each other even more as all of this is going on and feel more and more excited.

All this sounds exciting.

It sounds gross and messy. I don't want to hear any more about it.

When these feelings come to a climax, semen is ejaculated from the penis and spurts into the vagina, and the muscles in the vagina and uterus tighten and finally relax. This is called having an orgasm. Often, right after an orgasm, a small amount of fluid may come out of the vagina and out of the penis.

When two people, whether they are male and female or two males or two females, are having sexual intercourse, they may have orgasms at different times. And sometimes one person has an orgasm and the other doesn't. After an orgasm, most people feel relaxed, content, and sometimes even sleepy.

It's important to remember that the very beginnings of a new human being—a baby—can begin to form soon after or even a few days after vaginal intercourse between a male and a female, if and when a sperm

cell joins with an egg cell and plants itself inside the uterus. This can happen each and every time after vaginal intercourse unless the female is already pregnant or uses birth control, which can help to keep a female from becoming pregnant and having a baby.

People have a lot of mistaken ideas about how a pregnancy can begin. That's why it's important to know that a pregnancy can begin even if two people are standing up during vaginal intercourse, or if it is the very first time they are having vaginal intercourse. A pregnancy can also begin if two people have had vaginal intercourse only once, or if neither of them had an orgasm, or if a person is menstruating during vaginal intercourse.

A pregnancy can begin even if the penis is withdrawn from

We interrupt this program again to announce, "Baby-making warning! You can get pregnant if you have vaginal intercourse!"

Don't shout! I was trying to snooze!

the vagina before ejaculating. If sperm are ejaculated close to the opening of the vagina—or even if just a few sperm spurt out before ejaculation—it is possible for them to swim up the vagina and join with an egg. This can also happen when two people do not have vaginal intercourse, if sperm are ejaculated close to the opening of the vagina.

Waiting to have sex until one is old enough to take good care of a baby makes good

But why not?

Because I said no!

sense. The surest way not to become pregnant is to abstain from—not have—vaginal sex.

However, if a female and a male decide to have sexual intercourse, using birth control can be an effective way to help protect them from becoming pregnant and having a baby. And all couples—no matter who they are or with whom they are having sexual intercourse—can help protect each other from getting infections such as HPV, HIV, and gonorrhea that are spread by sexual contact if they use a new condom correctly and every time they have sexual intercourse. This is one way of practicing "safer sex."

There are other ways people make love and have sex. When a person puts their mouth on a vulva or a penis, this is called oral sex or oral intercourse. When an erect penis goes inside the anus, this is called anal sex or anal intercourse.

Some think that when people have oral sex or anal sex, they are not having sex—and that they are abstaining from sex. But having oral or anal sex is not a way of abstaining from sex. It is another way of having sex.

A pregnancy cannot begin after having oral or anal sex. But anyone—whatever gender or sex they may be—can get infections such as HPV, HIV, and gonorrhea, all of which are spread by sexual contact, by having vaginal or oral or anal sex. Using a new condom or barrier correctly and every time a person has vaginal or oral or anal sex is a way of practicing safer sex.

19
Before Birth
Pregnancy

The word *pregnant* comes from two Latin words: *prae,* which means *before,* and *gnas,* which means *birth.*

Pregnancy is the period of time before birth during which a fertilized egg plants itself inside the lining of the uterus, grows inside the uterus, and eventually develops into a baby. The union of a sperm and an egg is called conception or fertilization.

Scientists have discovered exactly how a pregnancy begins by observing how sperm travel, meet, and unite with an egg and how that united egg and sperm cell plants itself in the lining of the uterus.

Living sperm are great travelers, and it is wonderful to watch them move under a microscope. You can actually see their tails move rapidly back and forth. They look like tadpoles swimming and travel like a school of fish—in large groups of about five hundred million.

When sperm are ejaculated in the vagina during sexual

I wonder if sperm have races.

I know one thing for sure—there's usually only one winner in every race.

intercourse, they swim up the vagina, through the cervix, into the uterus, and into the fallopian tubes. If an egg is released and swept into one of the fallopian tubes, a sperm can unite with that egg and fertilize it.

Only about two hundred sperm out of the five hundred million in an ejaculation get close to the egg.

That's one out of every two million five hundred thousand sperm!

Hold on! I need my calculator.

Scientists have shown that a chemical in the fluid around the egg actually attracts certain sperm, telling them that the egg is ready, and lets only one sperm out of those two hundred or so break into the egg cell. After that sperm enters the egg, none of the others can get in, and fertilization takes place.

Once an egg cell unites with a sperm cell, it becomes a single cell—the first cell of a baby. A fertilized egg cell is called a zygote from conception and for the next several days as it travels to the uterus; an embryo during the next two months as it develops in the uterus; and a fetus throughout the rest of the pregnancy—until a baby is born. Some people call the fetus a "developing baby."

The fertilized egg cell takes about five days to travel through the fallopian tube and into the uterus, dividing again and again. Inside the uterus, which is also called the womb, the fertilized egg plants itself in the uterus's lining, where it can

THE FURTHER ADVENTURES OF THE EGG AND SPERM: *Pregnancy*

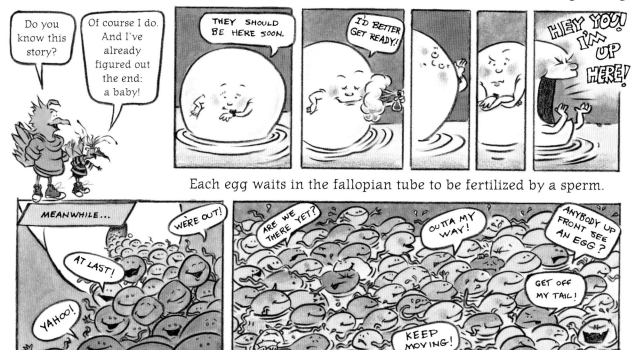

Each egg waits in the fallopian tube to be fertilized by a sperm.

Sperm leave the penis, swim up the vagina, through the uterus,

and into a fallopian tube, where an egg may be waiting to unite with a sperm.

If one sperm enters the egg, they become one cell and pregnancy can begin.

64 IT'S PERFECTLY NORMAL

start to grow and develop into a baby. This is when a pregnancy begins.

While in the uterus, a fertilized egg cell continues to divide billions and billions of times to make billions and billions of new cells. Eventually, over nine months, these cells become a whole new person—a baby.

In the uterus, a sac filled with a watery fluid forms around the developing baby and protects it against pokes, bumps, and jolts. The sac is called the amniotic sac or the "bag of waters," and the fluid is called amniotic fluid. This fluid is warm and keeps the developing baby warm as it floats.

A lot of kids and even some grown-ups think that the developing baby grows in the mother's stomach. It does not grow in the stomach.

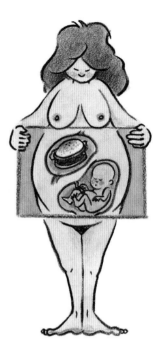

It grows in the uterus. As the developing baby grows bigger, the uterus also grows bigger.

As the embryo fastens itself to the inside of the uterus, a special organ called the placenta forms inside the uterus. During pregnancy, the placenta supplies the embryo and—later on—the fetus with oxygen from the air the

I wonder how long it takes a bee cell to grow into a bee.

21 days.

It takes a bird cell, depending on its cell size, anywhere from 10 to 74 days.

With the size of your birdbrain... I'd say 10 days.

Good. So the baby doesn't grow where the hamburger and ketchup go.

Thank goodness.

From Zygote to Baby—Nine Months

Zygote—*day 1*   Embryo—*month 1*   Fetus—*month 3*   Fetus—*month 6*   Baby about to be born—*month 9*

mother breathes and nutrients from the food she eats.

Nutrients are made up of vitamins, proteins, fats, sugars, carbohydrates, and water—all the things a fetus needs in order to grow into a healthy baby.

The umbilical cord—a soft, bendable tube—connects the placenta to the fetus at the umbilicus. The word *umbilicus* means *navel*, and *navel* is another word for *belly button*.

Oxygen and nutrients travel from the placenta to the fetus in the blood that flows through the umbilical cord. The oxygen and nutrients, as well as other substances from the mother, pass from her blood into the fetus's blood.

The fetus's waste—liquids and solids that are left over from the nutrients not used by the fetus—travel back through the umbilical cord to the placenta and pass into the mother's blood. The fetus's waste leaves the mother's body along with the mother's waste.

Medicines, drugs, and alcohol can also pass into the fetus's blood from the mother's blood. That's why people who are pregnant should be very careful about what they eat, and drink, and put into their bodies. If they need to take a prescription drug, they should check with their doctor or nurse to make sure the drug will not hurt the fetus.

If a pregnant person has been using substances like opioids, or consumes alcohol, smokes cigarettes, eats an unhealthy diet, or has certain kinds of infections while pregnant, this could affect the baby. Cigarette smoking during pregnancy can cause babies to be smaller at birth and to have other health problems as they grow up.

If a pregnant person has been addicted to drugs, including opioids, the baby will probably be smaller than expected, and might be born ahead of time. Infants born to

mothers who are addicted to opioids will need medical treatment, and some will need to stay in the hospital for a while.

"Addicted to opioids" means not being able to stop taking opioids. Pregnant women who receive medical help for their addiction to drugs while they are pregnant often do have healthier babies. Some of these babies are not born addicted to drugs. Some of the babies who are born addicted may do well. But all of these babies still need to have regular checkups to be examined by a doctor or nurse.

However, if a pregnant person has regular checkups with a nurse or doctor, eats healthy food, and gets enough exercise and sleep, that person's baby will have the best chance to be born healthy.

We're back to gross again.

Well, do you have a better suggestion?

20
What a Trip!
Birth

The birth of a baby is almost always a healthy and joyful event. A pregnant person knows that their baby is ready to be born when they can feel the muscles of their uterus tighten and squeeze and then relax, over and over, many times in a row.

These muscles are actually beginning to push the baby out of the uterus. All this tightening and squeezing and pushing is called labor. *Labor* is another word for *work*.

At some point after labor has begun, a pregnant person will usually contact their doctor or nurse or midwife to ask when it is time to go to a hospital or a birthing center. Others may go directly to the hospital without calling.

People who are pregnant may choose to have the birth of their baby at home. Most often their baby is born with the help of a doctor or a midwife and a nurse, who comes to the home after labor has begun and then stays for a while after the baby is born. A midwife—a person who has been specially trained

to help deliver a baby—is not a doctor but may be a nurse. The baby's other parent, or the mother's partner, and sometimes another family member or friend, can also help the mother during labor and birth. Labor can be as short as an hour or longer than a whole day.

After labor has started, and occasionally before, the amniotic sac— the bag of waters—breaks, and fluid begins to leak out. This can be another sign that the baby is ready to be born.

During the birth, the baby travels out of the uterus, through the cervix, which has opened and widened during labor, and into the vagina. The vagina stretches as the baby travels through the vagina and out of the mother's body. The vagina is often called the birth canal, because *canal* is another word for *passageway.*

What a trip!

Being born must feel sort of like a waterslide.

In most births, the baby's head pushes out of the vagina first. Any fluid in its mouth or nose is carefully taken out so the baby can breathe on its own. Then the rest of the body comes out. Usually the doctor, midwife, or the baby's other parent, or the mother's partner or other family member or family friend, gently holds the newborn baby as it comes out. This is called a vaginal birth.

When I arrived, I buzzed out.

I pecked my way out.

Some babies need to be gently guided out of the vagina. If so, the doctor may use a soft cap that is put on the baby's head. The doctor holds the handle of the cap and gently guides the baby through and out of the vagina as the mother pushes with the muscles of the uterus. This is called a suction birth. Some babies are gently

WHAT A TRIP!: *Birth*

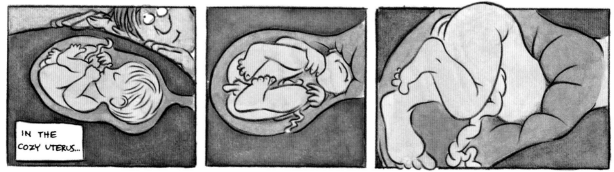

IN THE COZY UTERUS...

When it's time to be born, the mother's muscles squeeze and push the baby out

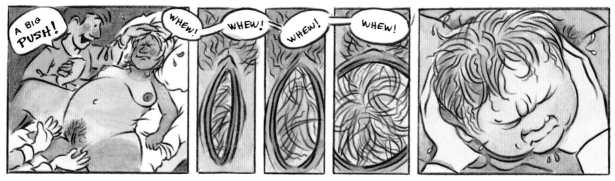

A BIG PUSH!

WHEW! WHEW! WHEW! WHEW!

and into the vagina. The vagina stretches wide and out comes

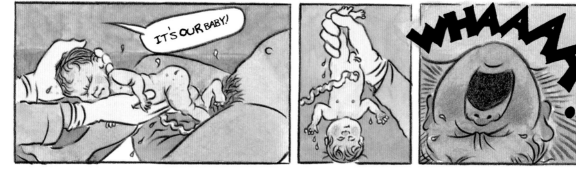

IT'S OUR BABY!

WHAAAA!

the baby, who is still connected to the mother by the umbilical cord,

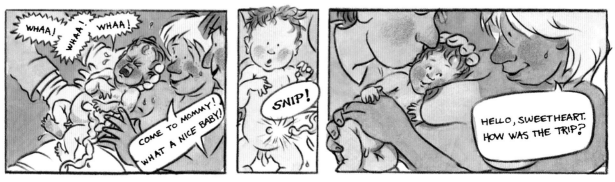

WHAA! WHAA! WHAA!

COME TO MOMMY! WHAT A NICE BABY!

SNIP!

HELLO, SWEETHEART. HOW WAS THE TRIP?

which is cut. And right away, the new baby is cuddled and held.

guided out by an instrument shaped like a pair of spoons called forceps as the mother pushes. This is called a forceps birth. Some babies come out of the uterus and vagina bottom first or feet first. This is called a breech birth.

Other babies are too big to travel safely through the vagina. Or they are in positions that make it difficult for them to travel out of the uterus and through the vagina on their own.

If the baby is too big or in an awkward position, the doctor makes a side-to-side cut through the mother's skin — after the skin and uterus have been made numb with a special medicine — into the mother's uterus and lifts the baby out and cuts the umbilical cord. Then the doctor takes the placenta out and sews up the cut, which heals in a few weeks' time.

This is called a cesarean birth, or C-section, and is another healthy way for a baby to be born. It is believed that the term *cesarean* dates back to the time of Julius Caesar, the great Roman leader, general, and politician, who may have been born this way around 100 BCE — more than two thousand years ago.

No matter which way a baby is born, right after birth it takes its first breath. This is also when most babies let out their first cry, which allows a baby's lungs to open up and begin to work on their own.

For many babies, as soon as the baby is born, the baby is given to the mother to hold against her soft, warm skin, even before the umbilical cord that has connected the baby to its mother during pregnancy is cut. Other babies are gently dried off; wrapped in a soft, warm blanket; and given to the baby's parent or parents to hold and cuddle after the umbilical cord is cut.

The moment a baby is born, even though the baby is still attached to the placenta by the umbilical cord, it does not need the placenta anymore. When the doctor or midwife cuts the umbilical cord, a clamp is

placed on the baby's umbilical cord and then the cord is cut about an inch away from the baby's navel. Since there are no nerve endings in the umbilical cord, neither the baby nor the mother can feel the cut. Sometimes the baby's other parent, or the mother's partner, or a family member or friend cuts the umbilical cord instead of the doctor or midwife.

A few days later, the clamped piece of umbilical cord dries out and falls off completely.

After the cord has been cut, the muscles of the uterus give a few more squeezes and pushes, and the placenta and amniotic sac slide out. Because they leave the mother's body after the baby has been born, they are called the afterbirth.

When parents are first given their newborn baby to hold and can feel the baby's skin against their skin and can feel the baby

I think I'll call you my adorable little Caesar.

breathe, they have—more often than not—new and special feelings of love and awe. These fond and loving feelings between parents and their child often begin at birth, but they can also begin in the weeks after birth.

I bet when my parents first laid eyes on me it was love at first sight.

I'm trying to picture that.

A few minutes after it is born, a newborn baby is usually weighed and measured and ointment is gently put into the baby's eyes to prevent infection. Within the first two days of birth, babies are also given a vaccine to prevent them from getting a serious illness called hepatitis B. Before new babies leave the hospital, most are given a shot of vitamin K to prevent them from getting a blood disease.

The birth of a baby is a fascinating event. At birth, a baby can see, hear, cry, suck, grab, feel, and smell. And it can eat by sucking from its mother's breast, which is called breastfeeding. Or a baby can suck its mother's breast milk from a bottle with a special top or suck a special milk made for babies called formula. A newborn baby can do an amazing number of things.

If a boy baby is to be circumcised, that is, if the foreskin of the penis is to be removed, either by a doctor or a person who has learned to perform circumcision as part of a religious ceremony, it is usually done a few days after birth. It takes only a few minutes to perform a circumcision.

Some circumcisions are performed for religious reasons. Baby boys born into the Jewish or Muslim faith are usually circumcised as part of a religious ceremony.

Other circumcisions are performed for health reasons to make it somewhat easier to keep the tip of the penis clean by washing it with soap and water so as to prevent infections. A baby boy's or a young boy's uncircumcised penis can also be kept clean by simply washing the penis with soap and water.

When boys who have an uncircumcised penis grow older, the foreskin separates from the tip of the penis. Once that happens, an uncircumcised penis can still be kept clean by gently pulling back the foreskin and washing the tip with soap and water while taking a bath or shower.

Some parents like the idea of having their male child look like the father, and sometimes that's how they make the decision about whether their baby boy is going to be circumcised.

Babies are born in many different ways. Some babies are born early, before they have spent a full nine months in the uterus. This is called a premature birth. A baby who is born early is called a premature baby or a "preemie."

A baby who is born only two or three weeks early has grown big enough to have a healthy start in life and can usually go home with its parents after one or two days in the hospital. But if a baby is born a month or more early, living outside the uterus can be hard. The baby's lungs may not be fully developed, making it difficult for the baby to breathe. The baby may not be able to suck or swallow easily, making it difficult for the baby to eat. And the baby may have trouble staying warm.

Babies who are born a month or more early usually have to stay in the hospital until they are healthy enough to go home. In the hospital, the baby stays in a specially equipped crib called an incubator, which keeps the baby warm and provides oxygen—just as the mother's uterus did for the fetus—while it continues to grow. While the baby is in the incubator, the baby's parents, the doctors, and the nurses feed and take care of the baby.

When the baby has grown big enough and is close to being as healthy as a baby who has spent a full nine months growing in the uterus, and can eat well and keep warm, its parent or parents can take their baby home.

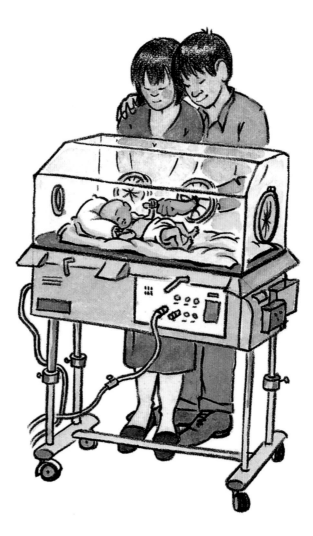

21
Other Arrivals
More Ways to Have a Baby and Family

Sometimes two people who have sexual intercourse want to have a baby but are not able to start a pregnancy. That may happen because their egg and sperm are not able to unite. Or it may happen because the two people may be the same sex. That means that their two bodies would only have eggs and no sperm—or that their two bodies would only have sperm and no eggs. And without an egg and a sperm, pregnancy cannot begin.

There can be many different reasons why an egg cell and a sperm cell are not able to unite. This can happen if too few sperm are traveling to the egg, or if the sperm are too weak to travel to the egg, or if the ovaries are not releasing an egg each month, or if the egg is unable to travel through the fallopian tubes.

Fortunately, there are ways other than vaginal intercourse to have a baby. With the help of a doctor, an egg can be fertilized by a sperm and a pregnancy can begin.

An egg can be taken out of one of the ovaries by a doctor and put into a small glass dish filled with liquid along with sperm that have been ejaculated. After the egg has been fertilized by one of the sperm in the dish, the egg is returned to the uterus, and a pregnancy can begin. This method of starting a pregnancy is called in vitro fertilization. *In vitro* are the Latin words for *in a glass.*

When a person's eggs cannot be fertilized, that person may choose to have an egg from another person's ovaries put into a dish with sperm so that the egg can be fertilized. The fertilized egg is then put into the first person's uterus so that a pregnancy can begin. This is called egg donation.

When there are not enough sperm, or not enough sperm strong enough to swim to the egg, a doctor can place ejaculated sperm in the vagina or uterus with a syringe. In the uterus, the sperm have a shorter distance to swim and a better chance of uniting with an egg in one of the fallopian tubes.

Starting a pregnancy this way, by placing sperm into the vagina or uterus, is called assisted insemination. *Inseminate* means *to put a seed in,* in other words, to make pregnant. *Assisted* means *to help.* This is also called alternative or artificial insemination—even though there is nothing artificial about the egg and sperm or the uniting of the egg and sperm. Instead, insemination is an alternative way—another way—to help a person become pregnant and give birth to a baby.

I could win any spelling bee with all these big new words.

That's only because you're a bee.

Sometimes, if a young male who has begun to make sperm or an adult male becomes very sick, the medication needed to be taken to become well may lessen the number of sperm that that person is able to make.

Before taking the medication, the male's ejaculated sperm can be placed in a sperm bank— a medical laboratory—to be frozen and stored for up to ten or fifteen years. It can be used later to conceive a baby by assisted insemination. Some healthy males also donate their sperm to a sperm bank to be used at a later date to help them or sometimes to help someone else start a pregnancy.

Sometimes, if a young female or adult female becomes very sick, that person's eggs can be removed by a doctor before taking any medication that is needed. The eggs are then frozen and stored and, if the female chooses, used later to conceive a baby by in vitro fertilization. A healthy female who wants to wait to have a baby may also choose to have

one's eggs frozen to be used at a later date to conceive a baby by in vitro fertilization.

Some females who are not able to conceive a baby may choose to have a surrogate pregnancy. One kind of surrogate pregnancy happens when an egg is removed from the uterus by a doctor, and placed with a sperm from a male, who may or may not be that person's husband or partner, in a small dish in a medical laboratory—where the egg and the sperm can meet and grow into an embryo. That embryo is then implanted in another woman's uterus, where it can grow into a baby. That person is called a surrogate. Another kind of surrogate pregnancy happens when the egg that joins with the donated sperm is the surrogate's egg.

Legal documents are made and signed before either of these processes start, so that when the baby is born, the baby goes home with and is the child of the two people whose egg and sperm, or whose surrogate's egg and sperm, first joined together to make that baby. Or the baby is the child of and goes home with the two women, or the two men, or the single woman, or the single man who has chosen to have a surrogate pregnancy as their way to have a baby.

There are people who are not able to conceive a baby at all—by sexual intercourse, by in vitro fertilization, or by assisted insemination. Or they do not choose to have a surrogate pregnancy. But they can start a family by adopting a baby or child.

Adoption means that a family will bring another family's baby or child into their family and raise that child as their very own. An adopted child becomes a member of his or her new family.

Many people choose to adopt children because they are not able to conceive a baby. Other people who can conceive a baby also choose to adopt children. Or a person may choose to adopt so they can become the other parent of a baby or children born to their partner.

Adoption usually occurs when a parent or parents who are unable to take care of their newborn baby or child decide to have someone else care for, bring up, and love their baby or child. Sometimes when two people are a couple, one of them may become pregnant and give birth to a baby. At birth, that parent automatically becomes the legal parent of that child. The other person in the couple may choose to adopt that child at birth or later. This is how the other person can also become the child's legal parent.

Adoption is a legal act. This means that the child's birth parent or parents sign a paper in front of a lawyer or judge that says that they are giving their child forever to a parent or parents who want to and are able to take care of the child. The new adoptive parent or parents agree to raise the child as their own. They too sign the adoption paper in front of a lawyer or judge.

There are many ways to have a baby and create a family. But no matter how people have a child, caring for and loving one can be a wonderful and amazing experience.

PART FIVE

Decisions

22

Planning Ahead
Delay, Postpone, Abstain, Prevent, Control

Whether or not to have sexual intercourse is a decision each person has a right to make. But a person should always remember that vaginal intercourse can result in pregnancy and having a baby. A person should also remember that vaginal, oral, or anal intercourse can result in a person becoming infected with a disease, even very serious diseases.

Many young people choose to wait to have sexual intercourse until they feel they are either old enough or responsible enough to make healthy decisions about sex. This is called postponement. *Postponement* means *to delay until a later time*. But the only sure way not to have an unwanted pregnancy is to not have vaginal intercourse. The only sure way not to get infected is to not have sexual contact with another person. The only sure way not to get infected is to abstain from having sexual contact with another person, which means to not have sexual contact with another person. To abstain from having sex is also called abstinence. *Abstinence* comes from the Latin word *abstinentia*, which means to decide not to do something—even something you may want to do.

Postponement and abstinence can prevent the start of a pregnancy and can also help prevent a person from getting or passing on infections that are spread by sexual contact. These kinds of infections are called sexually transmitted diseases or sexually transmitted infections. They are also called STDs or STIs for short.

Many people who choose to postpone or to not have sexual intercourse say that they can still have a close, loving, and sexy relationship with another person.

Sometimes, when people choose to have vaginal intercourse, they have planned to have a baby. But other people may want to wait to have a baby or may not want to have a baby at all. That's why knowing how to prevent pregnancy is important.

Birth control and *contraception* are the two names given to the many ways of preventing a pregnancy.

Contra is the Latin word for *against. Ception* is part of the word *conception,* which means *beginning. Contraception* means *against beginning a pregnancy.*

There are many kinds of birth control, and some work better than others. For most kinds, people must learn how to use them correctly and every time right before having sexual intercourse in order for them to work to prevent pregnancy. Even though using birth control correctly and every time is the most effective way to prevent pregnancy, no method of birth control can be guaranteed to work 100 percent of the time.

It's still important to know and remember that using any type of birth control can help to prevent a pregnancy and most often it does prevent a pregnancy. But using ANY type of birth control method without ALSO using a condom does not protect a couple from getting or passing on STDs—sexually transmitted diseases—to each other. STDs can be and often are very serious infections. That's why a couple must also use a condom. It's also important to know and remember that the best protection from becoming infected with a sexually transmitted disease AND from becoming pregnant is for a couple to use a condom WITH another type of birth control.

Condoms can be bought at a drugstore, a convenience store, or a supermarket. They are often

displayed in a special section or on the counter next to the pharmacy or near the cash register—and no prescription is needed. Condoms can also be bought online, and many health-care professionals will also provide them. All types of condoms work very well when used correctly.

A male condom is a soft, very thin cover that fits over an erect penis. When a male ejaculates, semen is kept inside the condom and sperm are not able to enter the vagina and unite with an egg.

Putting on a condom

Condoms are often called "rubbers" because they are usually made out of a rubbery material called latex. There are other types of male condoms made out of rubbery materials called polyurethane and polyisoprene. There are also condoms made out of lambskin.

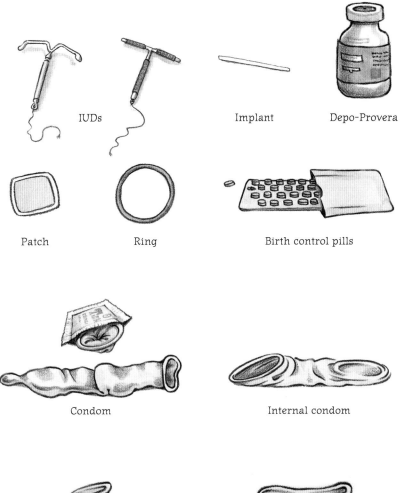

IUDs

Implant

Depo-Provera

Patch

Ring

Birth control pills

Condom

Internal condom

Cervical cap

Diaphragm

So condoms are rubbers.

But not like the ones you wear in the rain!

A condom designed to fit inside the vagina, called the internal condom and also known as the female condom, is often made out of a plastic material called synthetic nitrile. This soft pouchlike condom is inserted into the vagina before vaginal intercourse. This type of condom can also be inserted into the anus before having anal sex. However, a person may need a prescription from a health-care professional to buy an internal condom at a drugstore.

Using a new condom during vaginal intercourse, or oral intercourse, or anal intercourse, correctly and every time, can also help prevent the spread of infections—mild infections as well as life-threatening infections such as HIV and hepatitis B. This is a way of practicing safer sex. The most common infection that can be passed on is chlamydia. Although chlamydia is not life-threatening, it can cause infertility so that a female will not be able to become pregnant in the future and have a baby or a male is not able to make sperm. It's important to understand that any type of birth control method, when used by itself—*without a condom—cannot* prevent a person from getting an infection from or passing on an infection to another person.

It is also important to use condoms with silicone-based or water-based lubricants made especially for sex, and *not* made with oil. Oil can damage and break a latex condom.

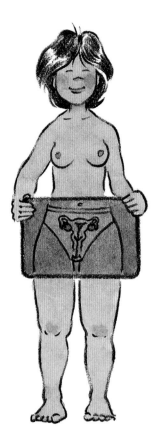

The IUD, the implant, and Depo-Provera, also called the shot, are the most effective kinds of birth control. Birth control pills, the patch, and the ring are almost as effective. Other kinds of birth control can also be effective, but are not quite as effective.

The IUD, the shot, the implant, birth control pills, the patch, the ring, the cervical cap, and the diaphragm are all contraceptives that a female can obtain only after talking with a trained health-care professional—a doctor, midwife, nurse practitioner, or physician's assistant—and obtaining a written prescription. The prescribed birth control method can then be obtained at a doctor's office or health clinic or purchased at a drugstore or from an online pharmacy. In some states, pharmacists can write a prescription for birth control.

Many birth control methods—the shot, some IUDs, the implant, birth control pills, the patch, and the ring—contain hormones. These hormones can keep the ovaries from releasing eggs so that there's no way for a sperm and an egg to join

Where They Fit

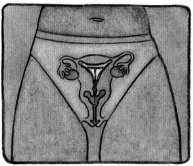

IUD

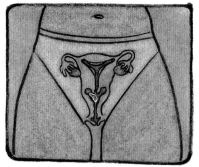

Ring

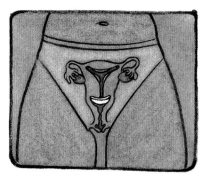

Diaphragm

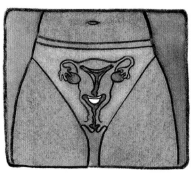

Cervical cap

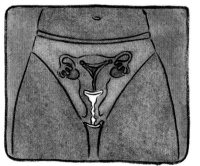

Internal condom

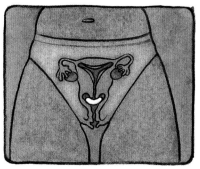

Sponge

together. These hormones can also make the fluid around the female's cervix thicker, which can also keep an egg and sperm from joining together.

An IUD, or intrauterine device, is a small plastic or copper device that is placed inside the uterus by a trained health-care professional and affects the way sperm move—so that sperm cannot swim to and join with an egg. The implant and the shot are birth control methods that contain artificial hormones that keep the ovaries from releasing eggs. The implant, a thin, flexible plasticlike rod about the size of a cardboard matchstick, can be inserted by a health professional under the skin of a female's upper arm and can stay in for five years. The shot is injected in a female's upper arm or buttocks every three months.

Birth control pills, commonly called "the pill," contain artificial hormones that keep ovaries from releasing eggs. A female must remember to follow the directions for taking a pill each day for this method to work.

The patch and the ring contain and release artificial hormones that can keep the ovaries from releasing eggs. The patch is a thin, square piece of plastic that sticks to the skin and looks like a bandage. It is placed by a

female on the skin of her upper arm, upper torso, stomach, or buttocks—but should not be placed on the breasts. Each week for three weeks, a new patch is placed on the female's body. The fourth week, no patch is used. The next month, the same process begins again. The ring is a small, soft, flexible plastic ring that a female can insert into the vagina. It is left in place for three weeks, and then is removed for one week. After that week, the female inserts a new ring.

The cervical cap and diaphragm are small rubbery cups that fit inside the vagina and are placed against the cervix before sexual intercourse. Both can prevent sperm from entering the cervix and traveling to the fallopian tubes. And both must be used with a spermicide.

Spermicide comes in different forms—foams, creams and jellies, and gels. The chemical in spermicide can kill sperm. Sponges containing spermicide may also block sperm and keep them from joining an egg. These kinds of contraceptives are inserted into the vagina before sexual intercourse. But they are not always able to kill, block, or catch every sperm and do not protect a person from getting or passing on an infection.

Spermicide should not be

used if a person is having intercourse often or having anal sex. Frequent use may cause irritation, which could increase the risk of infection. Spermicide and sponges can be bought at a drugstore, a convenience store, or a supermarket. They are often displayed in a special section, and no prescription is needed. They can also be bought online.

If there is an emergency and a woman or girl has been raped—forced to have sex against one's will—there are emergency contraceptive pills that can be taken to prevent the start of a pregnancy. These pills are also called "morning-after pills." They can also be used if a condom breaks, or is not put on properly, or a patch falls off, or if a female has unprotected sex for any reason. But they should not be relied upon as a regular form of birth control because there are many other kinds of methods that are more effective.

Morning-after pills contain hormones that are thought to delay ovulation and prevent the ovaries from releasing any eggs, so that pregnancy cannot begin. Some types of these pills must be taken within 72 hours — three days — after vaginal intercourse. Other types must be taken within 120 hours — five days — after vaginal intercourse. But they are more effective when taken as soon as possible after unprotected vaginal intercourse. However, any time a female has unprotected intercourse and does not want to become pregnant, she will need to take the pills again.

Some brands of the morning-after pill can be purchased by anyone of any age or gender and without a prescription at a local drugstore or online. There are also brands that can be purchased only with a prescription from a health-care professional. An IUD can also be inserted as a form of emergency contraception, and this must be done by a health-care professional.

Some methods of birth control, such as the withdrawal method or the rhythm method, which is also known as the calendar method, are not considered highly effective for preventing a pregnancy. It's also important to know that these methods of birth control cannot and do not prevent people from passing on an STD, a sexually transmitted disease — an infection — to another person. And they cannot or do not prevent a person from being infected by another person who has an STD.

When a female and male use the rhythm method, they try to figure out when the female's ovary has released an egg and then abstain from having vaginal intercourse during that time. However, it is very difficult to know when an egg has been released, because the time can vary from month to month — especially for many female teenagers.

When a male and female use the withdrawal method, the male withdraws the penis from the female's vagina just before ejaculation. This method does not work very well either because some semen may leak out before ejaculation or because males may fail to remove their penis before ejaculating.

Sometimes when people decide not to have more children, or decide not to have any children, they may choose to have a simple operation called sterilization.

When a male has this operation — called a vasectomy — a small piece of the vas deferens is removed or tied off by a doctor. As a result, the semen that is ejaculated no longer carries any sperm.

When a female has this operation — called a tubal ligation or a tubal sterilization — a small piece of each fallopian tube is removed or tied off or blocked by a doctor so that an egg cannot get to the uterus and sperm cannot get to an egg.

Some religions and groups and some individuals believe that using any method of birth control is wrong. Others believe that using the rhythm method and withdrawal method is fine. However, they also believe that using over-the-counter and prescription birth control methods is wrong.

I believe in planning. Each fall we birds plan to fly south.

But do you ever plan to stay south?

Still many others think birth control is a fine and responsible way to prevent an unwanted pregnancy or delay having a baby. These people use birth control to help them plan a family.

There are laws being voted on and policies being considered and enacted in some states and also by the federal government about contraception that could and in many instances do keep health-care professionals from giving information about contraception to kids and adults. This can mean that kids or adults who cannot get information about birth control may then become pregnant when they feel they are not ready, or are not old enough, or did not intend to have a baby.

Laws and policies can and do change. That's why it is important to talk with a trusted adult—a parent, doctor, nurse, psychologist, or another trusted adult—so that a person can get accurate information about contraception they want or need to stay healthy. Doing this can help kids and adults make the best and healthiest decisions about their bodies.

Your parent or parents, doctor or nurse, or other health-care providers are also good people to talk with about birth control, postponement, and abstinence. If you talk with a doctor or nurse or health-care provider, your talk will be confidential. Neighborhood health clinics or family planning clinics are also helpful places to go for information.

Okay! Talk to other people to get good info. Talking is what I love to do!

Not . . . okay. I love getting my info from all these books.

23

Laws and Rulings
Abortion

An abortion is a medical procedure performed for the purpose of ending a pregnancy. Some pregnant females choose to have abortions. People's feelings about having abortions are not always simple, however, and can range from relief to sadness, from worry to fear.

I've heard about abortion.

All I know is that people talk about it on the radio, on TV, and online too.

The word *abort* means *to stop* or *to end something at an early stage.* An abortion is usually performed in a clinic or a hospital by a doctor or other trained health-care professional and is a safe procedure, especially when done early in the pregnancy. The pregnancy is ended by removing the embryo or fetus from the uterus. The procedure itself takes about five minutes and is usually performed during the first three months of pregnancy, before most females even look pregnant. Sometimes abortions happen later. That's because at the moment, the laws of many states make it harder to get an abortion.

There are pills that can end a pregnancy and are used as another method of abortion. This method is called a medication abortion. The pills cause the lining of the uterus and the embryo to leave the female body. They can be taken by a pregnant female during the first ten weeks of a pregnancy. The first set of pills is taken at a doctor's office or clinic. The second set is usually taken at home one or two days later and followed by a checkup with a doctor or nurse.

These are some, but not all, of the reasons why people who are pregnant might want or need to end a pregnancy:
- They have an illness or inherited disease that makes the pregnancy or birth dangerous to their health and might even cause their death.
- A test shows that the fetus is carrying a serious inherited disease or a serious birth disability.
- They feel they are too young to take care of a baby in a responsible manner.
- They are sick and unable to take care of a baby.
- They do not have enough money or time to take good care of a baby or they already have children and cannot afford another child.
- They feel they are not ready to become pregnant.
- They are not in a good relationship or feel the relationship will not last and decide that having a baby under those circumstances would not be responsible.
- They were forced to have sexual intercourse against their will—raped—and became pregnant as a result.
- They are single and feel they are not able to raise a child on their own.

• They did not intend or want to become pregnant.

Sometimes the decision to have an abortion is made only by the woman or girl who is pregnant. Other times it is made jointly with another person such as one's parent or close family member or health-care provider or counselor or the person with whom one had sexual intercourse.

People have very strong feelings about whether or not a woman or a girl has the right to decide to have an abortion. In some countries, abortion is a right for all women and girls; while in others, the right to abortion is only permitted in some circumstances.

In 1973, the Supreme Court of the United States, which is the highest and most powerful court in the nation, ruled that a woman has the right to end an unwanted pregnancy. This ruling also says that no state can limit that right until very late in the pregnancy when the fetus could survive outside the womb. The court said it is up to each state how much to restrict abortion at this point in a pregnancy, so long as no restriction interferes with a woman's choice to end her pregnancy in order to preserve her own life or health.

The name of the 1973 Supreme Court decision is *Roe versus Wade*. Some individuals and groups are strongly for this decision and others are strongly against it.

People who support the Supreme Court decision favor a woman's right to decide whether or not to have an abortion. They believe that this is a deeply private and personal choice and should therefore be made by the individual female, not by the government.

People who think that this decision should be changed so that abortion is no longer legal—is no longer allowed—believe that the ruling allowing a woman to choose for herself whether or not to have an abortion is wrong. They believe that life begins when a baby is conceived and that an embryo or fetus has a right to life—a right to grow in a woman's body and to be born whether or not that woman wants to have a baby.

So people disagree . . .

I mean, you and I disagree, don't we?

But why can't people agree?

Because people believe in different things. Got it?

The rulings and laws about a woman's right to have an abortion have changed over the years and may continue to change. In 1992, the Supreme Court ruled to support their earlier 1973 decision guaranteeing a woman's right to decide whether or not to end a pregnancy. However, the court also ruled that any state in the nation may impose some restrictions on a woman's right to an abortion at any time during a pregnancy, but that it cannot outlaw abortion completely, or impose a substantial obstacle that can prevent a woman from getting an abortion.

Then in 2000, the Supreme Court again ruled to support a woman's right to have an abortion and made it clear that women, in consultation with their doctors, must be free to choose whatever method of abortion is safest for their health.

In 2007 the court reversed

course on that decision and further restricted the right to decide to have an abortion. It ruled that state governments and the federal government can prevent women from obtaining a specific method of abortion called intact dilation and extraction, as long as other methods are available. In this Supreme Court decision, *Gonzales versus Carhart*, the court upheld a federal law banning this method— even when doctors think it is medically the safest for women.

State governments have also made many laws that restrict and make it even more difficult for a female to get an abortion. For example, some states require that before an abortion can be performed,

• any girl under the age of eighteen has to have the consent of one or both of her parents or a judge's permission, depending on the laws of the state.

• a woman or girl must be told information by a health-care professional about alternatives to abortion, such as continuing the pregnancy and either keeping the baby and becoming a parent or giving the baby up for adoption.

• a woman or girl must first meet with a health-care professional about having an abortion and then wait twenty-four hours or longer before having one.

In addition, some states have passed other laws that can also restrict abortions for girls and women, such as,

• they cannot use medical insurance to pay for an abortion.

• they cannot obtain some types of safe abortion procedures.

• they cannot have an abortion performed after twenty weeks of a pregnancy, except when a girl or woman's life is at risk.

However, in some states laws have been passed that will keep girls and women from having an abortion performed after eighteen weeks, or twelve weeks, or even six weeks of a pregnancy, when a person might not even know they are pregnant. These laws are being challenged and most likely will continue to be challenged in the courts. But as of now, the United States Constitution gives women and girls the right to decide for themselves whether or not to have an abortion. That means that some of these laws that have been

passed by state legislatures may not go into effect.

There are also some states that have fewer restrictions. While many states have passed restrictions on abortions, some states have passed laws and other states are working on passing laws that will make it possible to have an abortion in their states. These state laws support a person's right to decide whether or not to have an abortion. If a person does live in a state that keeps them from having an abortion in their state, that person may be able to have an abortion in a state whose state laws have made it legal and safe to have an abortion. But if a person becomes pregnant and lives where they cannot get or where it is too difficult to get a safe and legal abortion, they may have no choice but to give birth to their baby.

However, in 2016, the Supreme Court ruled that there

are limits to the kinds of restrictions a state can place on abortion and that states must have good reasons and medical and scientific facts to pass any laws about abortion. This Supreme Court decision, called *Whole Woman's Health versus Hellerstedt*, also ruled that states cannot pass any laws to block abortion just because they do not like or approve of abortion. This decision made it possible for several health centers to continue to provide abortion and other health care that people, including kids and families, need.

Then, in 2020, the Supreme Court ruled that the reproductive health centers in the state of Louisiana can continue to provide abortion and other health care that people, including kids and families, need. This Supreme Court decision, called *June Medical Services versus Russo*, also ruled that since an identical case had already been decided four years ago in *Whole Woman's Health versus Hellerstedt*, this 2020 case had already been decided. However, if this law had been enacted, there would have been only one health center in Louisiana that would have been able to provide safe and legal abortions and other health care that people need.

But because laws can and do continue to change, it is likely that other abortion cases will be taken up in the future by the Supreme Court of the United States. That's why if a person needs information about abortion, it's important to ask a parent, teacher, doctor, nurse, psychologist, or other trusted adult what the laws and rulings about abortion are at this time, or what they are in one's state or nation.

It's also important to ask which health-care centers or clinics have trained health-care professionals who provide truthful, up-to-date, and accurate facts and information about abortion, or adoption, or anything else about one's health.

It SURE is important to know the truth.

It DEFINITELY is important to know the facts.

In fact, there are centers that tell people information that's not true, such as abortion causes cancer and mental illness or makes it not possible for someone to have a baby in the future. This information is false, and even though such centers may look like they are real health-care centers, they do not provide abortion care or offer any correct information about abortion. Usually, most of the staff at these centers are not real health-care professionals, even though they may dress like doctors or nurses and may wear lab coats to make it look like they are real health-care professionals. However, some centers have begun to have some health-care providers. But the goal of these centers still remains to convince pregnant women and girls not to have an abortion and instead to continue their pregnancy and give birth to a baby. This is intended to keep women and girls from making their own decisions about whether or not to continue their pregnancies. These centers now offer some health services, such as testing for pregnancy and sexually transmitted diseases, and a few of these centers now give out birth control. They also offer counseling and arrange for adoption. But their counseling still includes persuading people not to have an abortion and tells

people information about abortion and birth control that is not true. And they will not help a girl or woman get an abortion because they will not give them information on where and how to get a safe and legal abortion.

There are also centers called pregnancy counseling centers that clearly say that they are not health-care centers. They also say that they do not offer health-care services, but that they do offer pregnancy counseling and do give out baby supplies such as diapers, baby clothes, and baby toys. However, these centers also give out information about abortion that includes persuading people not to have a safe and legal abortion and tell people information about abortion that is not true. Some

also give out information about birth control and emergency contraception that is not true and is aimed to keep people from using birth control and using emergency contraception.

There are laws and policies being considered and enacted in some states and also by the federal government that can make it difficult or even impossible to get information about abortion or to have a safe and legal abortion. These laws and policies can and also do make it harder or even impossible for a person to make a decision about having an abortion. That's why it is important to talk with a trusted adult—a parent, doctor, nurse, psychologist, or another trusted adult—so that a person can get accurate information about

abortion. Doing this can help kids and adults make the best and healthiest decisions about their bodies.

Sometimes, usually during the early months of pregnancy, an abortion happens by itself, without a medical procedure. This is called a spontaneous abortion or a miscarriage. When this happens, the embryo or fetus is released from the mother's uterus without warning, often because it is not developing normally. Doctors do not always understand why miscarriages happen, but they know that females who have miscarriages can usually become pregnant again and give birth to healthy babies. The same is true for those who have chosen to have an abortion.

PART SIX

Staying Healthy

24

Helpful—Fun—Creepy—Dangerous
The Internet and You

Many kids, but not all, have a cell phone and keep in touch with their friends and family by sending texts, emails, posts, or even having a video chat. And many kids use cell phones, tablets, or computers to go online to contact others and to find information.

But it's important to remember that cell phones, tablets, and computers are just machines. And while these devices can provide good, fast ways to get information or to communicate with another person by texting, instant messaging, emailing, or contacting a friend online, they are not a substitute for actually being with a real person in real time. In fact, in every relationship and in every friendship, being with another person is very important.

It's also very important to know and remember that anything and everything you put in a text, or an email, or post online is there forever, and may not remain private if someone sends it on to or shares it with another person.

Chances are that you spend time online and that you already know that the Internet can be a great place to look up something you want to learn about or have questions or concerns about. You may also go online to watch videos, play games, get homework assignments, get help with homework, or to keep in touch with other people. Some of you may contact friends online by

going on a social network where friends can communicate with one another.

Information you may find on the Internet can be very useful. Going to websites and online encyclopedias and dictionaries can be a quick way to find information you are looking for. Searching for a word or topic online can also be helpful. Older kids and teens can find lots of responsible information online—including information about bodies, puberty, sex, gender, sexual orientation, and sexual health.

Here are some ways websites can be helpful. For example, if you are curious or have questions about puberty, pimples, the HPV vaccine, or cyberbullying, you can look up these and other topics online and learn about them. If other kids in your class have started having periods and you have not, or if you're the only kid in your class whose voice has changed, you can go online and most likely find out that not getting your period yet or that being the first one in your class to have your voice change is perfectly normal.

Information on the Internet about sex and bodies that is specifically written for older kids and teens can also help a person make good and safe decisions

about sexual health. That's because you can find facts on the Internet about topics such as the real risks of unprotected sexual contact, including pregnancy and the very real risk of being infected by a sexually transmitted disease. The Internet can also be a good place to check out if what you think you know or have heard about bodies or sex from your friends is true or not.

Searching the Internet is grrr-reat!

You could land somewhere so-ooo interesting . . .

Depends where you land.

or somewhere too-ooo creepy. . . .

Here are some things you need to think about when you go on the Internet.

There can be a lot of inappropriate, weird, confusing, uncomfortable, creepy, scary, or even dangerous websites that you can end up on when looking for information. This can happen if you end up on a website by accident, or on purpose, that has material you were not expecting.

While some of this information can feel exciting for kids and teens, it can also feel scary, upsetting, strange, gross, troubling, or puzzling. Often kids and teens have many of these feelings all at the same time, and that can also feel confusing or even disturbing.

Some websites are not always what they tell you they are. They are not real or responsible health or medical sites. And they could contain health or medical information that is scientifically or medically wrong, or information that is not up-to-date or not always true or correct. And some information online is fake.

Wrong or old or fake information can be harmful or even dangerous. It is not safe and it may not help you to stay healthy. And it can cause you to make decisions about your body and sex that are not healthy decisions for you or your friends. That's why it's very important to check with a trusted adult—your parent, or a teacher, librarian, therapist, school counselor, doctor, nurse, or clergyperson—to make sure the website you are going to or have just gone to has accurate, truthful, and up-to-date information that is based on scientific and medical facts.

Also, if you receive a text or email from someone you don't know or from a website you don't know or recognize, do not open what you received. Instead delete what you received and do not forward that text or email to anyone else as a way to keep others from receiving information that may be harmful or dangerous or not true.

If you happen to end up on a website and you see anything or read anything that makes you feel uncomfortable in any way, remember that you have not done anything wrong. You thought you were going to a responsible website and then you ended up somewhere else.

You may even find yourself on a site that has photos or videos of naked bodies or sexual acts that are created to make a person feel sexually excited.

These kinds of photos or videos are called pornography. Many people use the word *porn* as a short way of saying pornography. Some kids do not want to see these kinds of images at all. Other kids are curious about them and may find them exciting. Even so, people think that kids should stay away from porn.

In some cases, passing on some kinds of porn over the Internet to others can be risky and might be considered illegal. That's one reason why it's also important to talk to a trusted person if you end up on a porn site—no matter why or how you ended up on that site.

Whether you happen to end up on one of these sites, or on any site, by accident or on purpose—if what you see is upsetting, scary, confusing, gross, and/or weird, or more than you ever want to see about bodies or sex, and makes you feel uncomfortable, leave that site right away. And talk with a person you know and trust right away. Talking with someone about what you saw and how you feel can be very helpful.

Usually, but not always, the people in these photos or videos are actors, who are not having caring, loving, real relationships, and are not having relationships in which they treat each other with respect. What is important to know and understand is that what really matters in any relationship involving sex is that people treat one another in respectful, caring, and loving ways.

No matter what, if you ever find yourself in an inappropriate or uncomfortable situation while you are on the Internet, always remember that you don't need to look at or read what is online, whether you have gone there by mistake or because you thought you wanted to be there.

And if you read something in a text or receive an email that worries you in any way, do not reply. Instead, talk with a responsible and trusted person about what you just saw or read.

That person can be a parent and, if at school, the principal. And make sure you talk with someone right away, especially if the email worries or scares you.

Here are some rules to think about when you go online to talk to or meet someone through a social network site. Following these rules can help you protect yourself.

- Every time you use a cell phone, a tablet, or a computer, the most important thing to think about is your privacy and safety and that of your family, friends, and classmates. And whenever you set up privacy settings, it's a good idea to check in with a parent or trusted adult to help you make sure you have set up your settings in a way that protects you.
- You may think that certain sites are privacy protected, but many are not. This means that it is possible that people you know and even strangers could see posts you do not want them to see—posts you thought were private and wanted to keep private. So be sure to check the privacy settings on any site you go on.
- Only friend people you know. It is also extremely important to make sure that you use

privacy settings to make sure that information from and about you is blocked from everyone except people on your online friends list. And if someone sends you a text or emails you and that person says and pretends to be a friend or to know you, but has a screen name you do not recognize, then block that screen name so that person cannot contact you again.
- Do not post any private details about yourself, such as your age, gender, telephone number, street address, the name and street of your school, or where you are going, to anyone whom you do not know, when you visit a social network site on the Internet. If anyone asks you questions that you do not want to answer, do not answer them, and immediately tell a trusted adult. And never give anyone your password.
- If you get a call or text on your phone and you do not know who sent it or do not recognize the telephone number, do not answer that call or open that text. Delete it from your phone.
- Do not have conversations with or arrange to meet someone who contacts you online whom you do not know

in person, even if a friend knows that person or if the person is someone from your school whom you've never met. The same rule applies if someone you don't know sends you a text or an email and tries to get you to come and meet them in person. Some strangers who contact you online could be grown-ups pretending to be kids as a way to get you to meet them. You cannot know for sure who a stranger on the Internet really is. It's even possible that you could be physically hurt by a stranger. You need to tell a trusted adult immediately if a stranger ever contacts you online and asks to meet you in person, even if the stranger tells you to keep this a secret. Finding and telling a trusted adult can help you to stay safe.

We definitely know it's definitely NOT safe if a stranger tries to meet you.

DO NOT do it! It's TOTALLY dangerous!

Sending sexual messages, photos, or videos to someone over the Internet is called *sexting*,

which is a combination of two words—*sex* and *texting.* In some states, sexting may be considered a crime. That is one more reason to be extremely careful about what you decide to send someone via the Internet. It matters that you know that what you send may not remain private and what that could mean for you and your friends and family—especially something that might be considered sexting. Thinking about this may help you to decide not to text, post, or send something that is private about you and/or your body or about any friend.

Never send over the Internet or post videos or photos of you or your family or friends on the Internet that you would not want your parent or teacher or principal to see. Never text, email, or post or copy a video

or photo of yourself, or any part of your body, even if you think sending a picture of your belly button or a picture of you in boxer shorts or in polka-dot underpants is funny. Why not? Someone can send this video or photo to all of your classmates, even to other schools and all around the world. If just one person sends it on, it can go anywhere on the Internet, to anyone else's cell phone, tablet, computer—to other kids, to your parent, or even to your teacher or the principal of your school, and even to strangers.

The same thing is true with words you may text, email, or post via the Internet. Behave as carefully online as you would in everyday contact with another person. Before you say something mean about someone or get angry with someone in a

text message, post, or email, think twice before sending those strong words.

Once your words are on the Internet, they are there forever, and you cannot get those words back. Others whom you do not want to see those words may end up seeing them. There is no way to guarantee that what you have sent will remain private.

If you say online that someone is fat or skinny or sexy or ugly or beautiful or handsome, what you have said is really never private once those words are on the Internet. Saying something mean, or bullying someone, or spreading any kind of gossip, even sexy rumors or gossip, about another person, can make that person feel really crummy, or extremely sad or angry, and can hurt that person's feelings a lot. When someone does this online by sending a text, post, or email, it is called cyberbullying. To *bully* means to *mistreat another person. Cyberbullying* means *mistreating another person online.*

Nobody should ever bully anybody online. It's MEAN! It's a HORRIBLE thing to do!

Nobody should ever bully anybody in person either. It's AWFUL! It's a TERRIBLE thing to do!

It's very important to remember to treat others with kindness and respect when online and in person, and to treat others the same way that you want to be treated.

You may have heard the phrase "hate speech." This kind of speech is one of several ways people cyberbully. Hate speech means saying or writing words to or about another person or group of people that insults that person or group because of who they are. Often, but not always, hate speech is based on a person's sexual orientation or gender identity, looks, race, or religion.

Many parents and schools have rules about using cell phones and the Internet. Many schools have forms to sign to make sure you follow their rules when on the Internet or on a cell phone. These rules and forms are not about keeping you from finding information online or from being in touch with friends. These rules are about keeping you safe, and often they include never cyberbullying anyone you know or don't know—anyone at your school, in your neighborhood, or on a team with you, or anyone who is younger or older than you.

Parents and teachers have these rules and forms to keep you safe—whenever you use a cell phone, tablet, or computer.

You may wonder, safe from what? Parents, teachers, and librarians are afraid that you will end up on a website that might upset or possibly harm you, and they want to stop either of those things from happening to you.

These rules can help keep you safe whenever you are online or on your cell phone. And they can help make sure that any private information about you stays private, so that strangers cannot contact you or meet you.

Every family and school may feel differently about cell phones and the Internet and may have different rules. It's important to talk with your family about their rules and to also find out what the rules are in your school, so that you do stay safe.

Finding healthy information and staying safe on the Internet is something most everyone can do. But if you need help or come across information that's upsetting, or if someone online whom you don't know tries to meet you in person—make sure you go and talk to an adult you trust. That adult can help you to stay both healthy and safe.

Going online can be useful and interesting because of the many wonderful and responsible websites that can help you find the information you are looking for—or new or different information that you may find by chance.

The information you find on responsible websites can turn out to be helpful to you by answering questions or addressing concerns you may have about sexual health. It can also help you think about yourself and your friends in new and caring ways as you are growing up and going through puberty and adolescence.

25

Talk About It
Sexual Abuse

It's sad but true that some people's sexual behavior can be dangerous and even hurt others. This kind of behavior is called sexual abuse.

Do we have to hear about sexual abuse?

I think we do.

Sexual abuse is a subject that kids and adults find very hard and painful to think about and talk about. People often hear a lot of wrong and confusing things about it.

Though most kids have probably heard the words *sexual abuse*, that doesn't mean they know exactly what those words mean. *Sexual* means *having something to do with sex*. *Abuse* means *to treat wrongly, to mistreat*.

Sexual abuse happens when someone mistreats another person in a sexual way. Sometimes it happens when someone who is more powerful than another person or when someone who is older than another person takes advantage of that person in a sexual way. It is wrong for anyone to take advantage of another person just because a person is older or more powerful.

But there is more than one kind of sexual abuse. Most of us—kids and grown-ups—are taught rules as we are growing up about treating others with respect. Sexual abuse happens when someone breaks the rules that have to do with another person's body. When someone talks about or makes unwanted or inappropriate sexual comments to another person about that person's body—that's one kind of sexual abuse.

Sexual abuse is also about any kind of unwanted sexual contact, from touching to kissing to sexual intercourse. This happens when someone touches or does something to the private parts—the sexual parts—of another person's body that that person does not want them to do, or when someone makes another person do something to a person's private parts that that person does not want to do.

This someone can be someone the person knows, someone the person loves, or a stranger. The truth is that it is most likely, but not always, someone the person knows. Sexual abuse can happen between kids and adults—even between a parent and a child. It can also happen between one kid and another kid or between a brother and a sister. It can happen to kids, no matter what their gender may be. It can also happen to adults.

The usual and normal daily hugging, kissing, touching, and holding hands that go on among family members and good friends because they care about one another are not sexual abuse. A doctor's or nurse's physical examination of a person's body is part of the regular checkup kids and adults need to stay healthy. When kids get injured in sports, often a physical therapist, or a coach, or other adults may need to help you to recover.

But if any of these adults or any other person says any words or touches you in any way that makes you feel uncomfortable, do not wait to tell an adult you trust that this has happened. Tell someone you trust as soon as you can, so that trusted adult can help to keep this from happening to you again.

Sexual abuse can feel painful or even hurt a lot. But not all sexual abuse hurts. In fact, a person can be abused in a way that can feel loving and gentle. When this happens, a person can feel very confused, because it's almost impossible to understand how something so wrong can feel gentle or loving.

In any sexual touching or sexual relationship, both people—even if one person is stronger or older or more powerful than the other person and no matter what gender they are—have the responsibility to have a caring, thoughtful, and respectful relationship with the other person. All kids, all people, must respect one another by not coercing—which means forcing—the other person to engage in any type of sexual relationship, even when one's sexual feelings are very strong.

Whether sexual abuse hurts or feels gentle or even loving, it is always wrong. People, especially grown-ups, know it is wrong. It is not your fault if it happens to you. Even if kids do not know the rules, grown-ups do or should know the rules.

Before anyone touches any part of a person's body, unless it is one's nurse or doctor during a medical checkup, a person must have the other person's consent—permission—to touch their body. If a person touches any part of another person's body without their permission, that is abuse. If that person touches any of the sexual parts of another person's body without their permission, that is sexual abuse. If a person is forced to have sexual intercourse against their will, that is called rape. Rape is sexual abuse. Rape is also against the law, and people who commit rape often end up going to jail. That is because they have committed a crime. In fact, all kinds of sexual abuse are crimes.

It is important always to remember that your body belongs to you. It's also important to know there are lots of people around who do care about kids and want to keep them safe.

If anyone tries to do something to your body that you don't want them to do or don't think they should do, say, "NO!" or "STOP!" or "DON'T!" to the person who is abusing you.

Some of you may have heard the word *harass. Harass* means *to annoy* or *bother.* If anyone harasses or bothers you by talking about sex, by using rude or dirty words about sex when you don't want them to, or by talking about your body in a way that you don't like—tell that person to STOP! This kind of harassment is called sexual harassment. Even though that person is not actually touching your body, talking about sex or your body in this way is another kind of sexual abuse.

Sometimes a person will try to tempt another person to engage in sex by flirting or telling a person how pretty or handsome they are, or by dressing in a sexy manner. This can feel very confusing because there are times that these kinds of behaviors are fine and normal. But sometimes they are not fine or normal *at all* and can even include offering a person alcohol or drugs—even when that person is too young—or

showing that person photos or videos of naked bodies.

These kinds of behaviors are *wrong* and *inappropriate,* and they can happen to both kids and adults. If this ever happens—tell that person, "STOP!" And then go and tell a trusted adult immediately what has happened, so that the adult can help to make this stop. This too is a type of abuse.

There are some secrets with a trusted friend that are okay to keep. But don't keep any kind of sexual abuse a secret if it happens to you or to a friend—even if someone tells you to keep it a secret. Tell another person you know and trust—right away!

If the first person you tell doesn't listen to you, tell a second person. Talk about it until you find someone who understands you and believes you. That person will help you.

Sometimes some kids, and even some adults, find it difficult to go by themselves to talk with and tell someone they trust that they have been sexually harassed or sexually abused. If so, one can ask a good friend or friends to help them not only find a trusted adult but also go with them to talk with that trusted adult.

This is a way of helping a friend—a way of saying, "I want to help you" or "We want to help you." And often that trusted adult can help or find a person who can help to make the abuse stop.

Sometimes people wait for a while or for a long time to tell another person that they have been abused. Even if you have waited and then decide to tell a trusted adult that you have been abused, it's still important to get help as soon as you feel you are able to from a trusted person or health-care professional with whom you can talk to about what happened to you.

Always remember, if someone abuses you, it is NEVER your fault!

You also should never abuse anyone in any way. It's not fair. It's not your right. When someone says NO to you, you must believe that person and honor that person's wishes.

Most people don't like to talk about sexual abuse, but now a lot more people are talking about it. A kid can talk about it with a parent or a friend or a teacher. Very often it helps to talk with a therapist, school counselor, doctor, nurse, or clergy member—people specially trained to help. When people, including kids, who have been sexually abused can talk about the abuse with someone they trust, they may eventually feel better because they have been able to talk with someone they trust. Talking can or may help a person understand and know that what happened to them is not their fault and that they did nothing wrong. It was the person who abused them that did something that was wrong—very wrong. It's okay to talk about being abused only with someone you trust. It's also okay to talk about and speak out to others about being abused.

It's scary and creepy to hear about sexual abuse.

Yes, it is. But I do feel better just talking about it.

26
Getting a Checkup
Sexually Transmitted Diseases

Sex is usually a healthy, natural, and perfectly normal part of life. But sometimes sexual activities can be unhealthy.

Sexually transmitted diseases—called *STDs* for short—are diseases, infections, or illnesses that can spread from one person to another through sexual contact, from sexual touching to any kind of sexual intercourse—vaginal, oral, or anal intercourse. Another term for STDs is *STIs*—short for *sexually transmitted infections.*

Infections and diseases such as colds and flus are caused by germs, which are so tiny they can be seen only by looking under a microscope. Not all germs cause sickness. But some germs, including some viruses and bacteria, do. Germs can be passed from one person to another by all sorts of contact—such as sneezing, shaking hands, and using the same glass, plate, or silverware.

STDs are different from most other infections—different from colds or the flu—because they are spread by sexual contact. A person who is having sex should be tested every year at a health clinic or doctor's office to see whether or not they have an STD. If a person does have an STD, knowing that means that they can go to a health-care professional to find out if there is a medical treatment that can help them feel better or even in some cases cure their disease. Some people do not like to talk about STDs because they may feel embarrassed or worried about STDs. But talking about and learning about them is important for your health.

I don't even like to hear about any diseases at all.

Me neither, but we'd better listen.

There are many STDs. Some are not very serious. Others can be extremely serious. They can cause people to become infertile. If a person is infertile, that means a person is not able to make sperm or that a person is not able to become pregnant or stay pregnant. This can mean that a person's sperm and a person's egg are not able to meet and therefore a pregnancy cannot begin.

STDs can also cause death. But many STDs can be cured. And there are medicines and treatments that can make a person feel better if that person has one of the STDs that cannot be cured.

Germs are not the only way a person can get an STD. A few STDs, such as pubic lice and scabies, are caused by tiny bugs.

Pubic lice are a fairly common STD. You may have heard people call lice "crabs." That's because lice are tiny six-legged bugs that look like crabs. Pubic lice like to live in warm, hairy spots, like the pubic area, and are passed on through sexual contact. Pubic lice can be easily cured by putting a medicine, which kills the lice, on the pubic area. These lice are different from common head lice, because head lice are not transmitted from one person to another by sexual contact. Head lice are not an STD.

Scabies can be, but is not always, an STD. It is caused by tiny bugs called mites that can cause severe itching in the areas around a person's genitals, as well as other parts of the body, except the neck and head. Scabies can be treated by putting medicine on the infected area.

Sometimes we have to hear about diseases.

Even if we don't want to hear about them.

Sexual contact is not the only way a person can get lice or scabies; contact with an infected person's sheets, towels, or clothing can also pass them on.

Chlamydia, gonorrhea, and syphilis are three STDs that are caused by bacteria. They can usually be cured by going to a doctor or a clinic and taking the correct medicine. However, if these STDs are not treated, a person can become very sick and lose his or her sight or the ability to have children. A mother who has one of these STDs can pass it on and cause damage to her newborn baby.

Often people who have chlamydia or gonorrhea might not know they are infected because they do not feel sick. But there are medical tests that can be given to determine if a person has one of these infections. Females can and should be tested for chlamydia from the first time they have sexual intercourse and every year up through the age of twenty-six. Syphilis is an extremely dangerous STD, and if not treated can result in death. If a test shows that a person has chlamydia, gonorrhea, or syphilis, that person and their partner should start medical treatment by a doctor or nurse as soon as possible.

Hepatitis is caused by a virus that infects a person's liver. There are many different kinds of hepatitis. Medical tests can determine if a person has hepatitis.

Hepatitis B is an STD that is very contagious. It can be passed on during sexual intercourse and by using unclean needles and syringes. People who take drugs by using or sharing unclean needles and syringes are at a high risk of getting this STD. If you have your ears pierced or get a tattoo, you must make sure that a brand-new, germ-free needle is used. There is no cure for hepatitis B, but there is a vaccine that can keep a person from getting the virus. A pregnant woman or girl can pass the virus on to the new baby during birth. All new babies, and any person under age eighteen who has not been vaccinated, should be vaccinated to keep them from getting hepatitis B. Most people who get this virus get well, but it can result in cancer or death.

Hepatitis C can also be spread by sexual contact and passed on by the use of unclean needles and syringes. There is not yet a vaccine for hepatitis C that can be taken to prevent someone from getting the virus. But scientists are working hard to create a safe and effective vaccine. However, there are treatments a person can take, including pills, which can make it possible for someone who has hepatitis C to be cured.

HPV infection, an STD caused by a virus called human papillomavirus, is very contagious and can cause cancer, including cancer of the cervix. It can also cause genital warts. HPV can be spread from one person to another person by sexual contact. A vaccination—a series of two shots—can be given to kids between the ages of nine and fourteen. The second shot is given at least six months after the first. It is recommended that kids be given the shot as soon as age nine. It is effective if given when a kid is younger. If older than fourteen, it is recommended that three shots be given within six months of each other. This vaccine prevents kids and many adults from getting or passing on HPV and also prevents kids and many adults from getting some kinds of cancers, including cervical cancer.

The vaccine works best before the person has any kind of sexual contact. It can be given to anyone of any gender up to the age of twenty-six.

In some cases HPV goes away on its own. Some kids and some adults can feel genital warts—bumps or growths—on or around their genitals or anus. They may also feel itching. Most do not feel either and do not know they have genital warts. That's why it's important to have regular checkups. A Pap smear test can determine if a female has HPV on the cervix. A medicine can be applied on the cervix to remove the warts or they can be removed by a doctor.

Herpes simplex virus causes an infection that can be, but is not always, sexually transmitted. This virus is passed on from one person to another by skin-to-skin contact and is extremely contagious. Herpes simplex virus can also be spread by saliva.

Herpes 1 causes blisterlike sores to form on or near a person's lips, mouth, nose, and eyes. Herpes 2, or genital herpes, causes blisterlike sores to form on or near a person's genitals and anus. Often people do not know that they have herpes. There are medical tests that can determine if a person has herpes. No cure has been found for the herpes simplex virus, but both types can be treated by a doctor with medicine that can make the sores go away and make the infected area feel better. However, the sores can come back. A pregnant woman or girl can pass the virus to the baby during birth.

It is mostly adults and teenagers who get STDs. If a person has sexual contact, using a new condom correctly and every time can help protect him or her from getting or passing on some of these infections. This is one way of practicing safer sex. Unprotected sex is extremely risky.

Condoms are the only contraception that can help to protect one from getting an STD or passing on an STD to another person. Abstinence is the surest way to protect oneself from getting infected by a sexually transmitted disease.

Not all infections are caused by sexual contact. But if a person feels discomfort or pain on or near any of the sexual parts of their body, it is important to tell their parent, or the school nurse, or another trusted adult, so that a health checkup can be arranged. If a person has a sexually transmitted disease, getting prompt medical care may make that person feel better. It may also save a person's life, as well as stop the spread of the infection to another person.

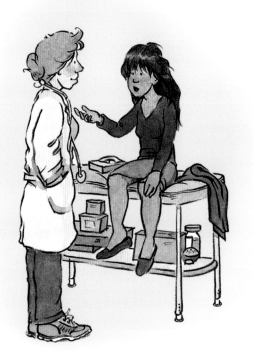

27
Scientists Working Day and Night
HIV and AIDS

HIV infection is a sexually transmitted disease and is one of the most serious of all STDs. HIV is the germ—the virus—that causes AIDS. If a person is infected with another STD, that person has a high risk of becoming infected with HIV as well. However, many people who have HIV, and who take their medications regularly and have regular checkups with their doctors or nurses, can and do live healthier and longer lives.

The letters *HIV* stand for *human immunodeficiency virus*—the scientific term for the AIDS virus, HIV. A *virus* is a type of germ—too small to see without a microscope—that can cause a person to become sick. The letters *AIDS* stand for *acquired immunodeficiency syndrome*—the scientific term for AIDS. *Acquired* means *something you can get. Immunodeficiency* means not able to protect against or fight infections and cancer. *Syndrome* means *a group of symptoms or conditions that may accompany an illness or a disease.*

What HIV and AIDS mean is that when people who are infected with HIV develop AIDS and become sick, their bodies are no longer able to protect against or fight infections and cancer. Scientists and doctors know that most people who are infected with HIV and do not receive treatment will eventually develop the symptoms of AIDS. These include coughing, fevers, weight loss, swollen glands, diarrhea, and being unable to think or see clearly. A person who has HIV infection may not get sick for a long time, as long as ten years or more. However, most people who develop AIDS and do not receive anti-HIV drugs eventually die from one or more of its symptoms or conditions.

At this time, there is no cure

for AIDS. But there are some medicines that can slow down the virus and keep it from spreading in the body for many years. These drugs are helping people who are infected with HIV to feel healthier and live long lives.

Any person can get HIV infection—young or old, rich or poor, straight, famous or not famous, weak or strong. Any person of any race, gender, or religion can get infected with HIV and can develop AIDS. HIV infection has nothing to do with who you are; it can have a lot to do with what you do.

A blood test that doctors and nurses perform shows whether a person has been infected with HIV. If a person has the virus, that person could remain healthy and lead a good and productive life for many years. Without the blood test, it is not easy to know if the virus is in a person's body.

The term *HIV positive* means that a person has HIV infection in their body. But scientists and doctors have learned a lot about HIV and have discovered ways a person *cannot* get HIV infection—and ways a person *can* get HIV infection.

How can you get HIV?

How can you *not* get HIV?

Ways you *cannot* get HIV infection

- You cannot get HIV from playing tag, wrestling, hugging, shaking hands, giving a friendly kiss hello, or giving a high-five to a person who has HIV.
- You cannot get HIV from food, a plate, a doorknob, a comb, a brush, or a toilet seat that a person with HIV has touched.

- You cannot catch HIV the way you catch a cold, because the germ or virus does not travel through the air. That means you cannot get HIV from a cough or a sneeze.
- You cannot get HIV from donating blood.
- You cannot get HIV from a mosquito or flea bite.
- You cannot get HIV just by being in the same room with someone who has HIV. That means you cannot get HIV just by going to school with someone who has HIV.
- You cannot get HIV by swimming in the same pool with someone who has HIV.
- You cannot get HIV from visiting someone who has HIV at home or in the hospital.

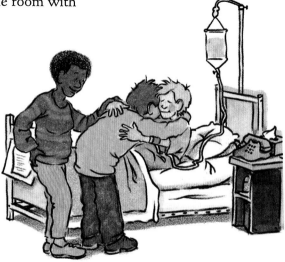

I like hearing about all the ways you cannot get HIV.

Me too. But I do wonder how you can get HIV.

Ways you *can* get HIV infection

- You can get HIV from a person who has the virus either from semen from the male's penis or fluids from the female's vagina. These body fluids carry HIV. That means you can get HIV from having sexual intercourse with a person who is infected with the virus even if that person appears to be healthy.
- It also means that if a person has vaginal sex, oral sex, or anal sex with someone who has HIV, and does not protect themselves correctly and every time, there is a real risk of getting infected with HIV. This is why it is important to ask one's partner or let one's partner know if either person is infected with HIV. If a person chooses to have sex, using a new condom every time a person has sex can help protect people from getting HIV. Unprotected sex is extremely risky.
- You can get HIV from the blood of a person who has the virus. That means you can get the virus if the blood from a person infected with HIV enters your bloodstream— or if blood that has HIV in it is injected into your body. However, all blood donated for kids, babies, and adults who need blood in a hospital or at home is tested to make sure it does not have HIV in it before it is given to them.
- You can get HIV if you take drugs by using a needle and syringe that has been used by a person who has HIV. People who take drugs by using unclean needles and syringes or sharing needles run a big risk of getting HIV.

People have to be careful.

They sure do.

But every time you get a shot from your doctor or nurse to keep you healthy, a brand-new, disposable, clean, germ-free, sterile needle and syringe are used and then thrown away in a safe place. You cannot get HIV from brand-new, germ-free needles and syringes. If you have your ears pierced or get a tattoo, you must make sure that the needle used is brand-new, germ-free, and disposable.

- A female who has HIV can pass the virus to her fetus while it is in her uterus, or to her baby during birth. That is why some babies are born with HIV. But a pregnant female who has HIV can take a daily medicine that can keep the virus from entering the baby's body and keep the baby from being born with HIV.

It's good that medicine can help.

Very good!

- Some mothers who have HIV can pass the virus on to their babies through the milk from their breasts. (This is called

breastfeeding). Instead, a baby can drink a special drink from a bottle, called formula, which has some milk, vitamins, minerals, and sugar in it.

Luckily, scientists and doctors have discovered ways in which people can protect themselves from getting HIV and lessen their chances of developing AIDS. One way is to abstain from having sexual intercourse with another person. This is called abstinence and is the only fully safe way people can protect themselves from getting HIV through sexual contact.

If a person chooses to have sexual intercourse, using a male or female condom can lessen the chance of getting HIV infection. Using a new condom correctly and every time is one way people are practicing safer sex. Not sharing needles is another way to avoid the chance of getting HIV infection.

Scientists all over the world are working day and night in laboratories to try to make a vaccine that will prevent a person from being infected with HIV if that person comes into

contact with the virus. Just as there are vaccines to protect people from being infected with measles, mumps, or polio, an HIV vaccine could prevent a person from being infected with HIV and developing AIDS.

Scientists have also developed and are still working on developing even more pills, shots, or other treatments that they hope will help people who already have the virus to lead longer and healthier lives. They hope that such treatments will either keep the virus quiet so that it will not be able to harm a person or eliminate the virus from a person's body entirely. Sometimes, these treatments for HIV can make the infected person feel sick. That's why scientists are also working to develop medicines and treatments for HIV that can help make an infected person feel less tired or less uncomfortable.

But even without a vaccine or treatment, people can help protect themselves from getting HIV infection by knowing how the virus is passed from one person to another.

Many people who are HIV positive or who have developed AIDS are able to go to work or school and carry on with most parts of their lives for a number of years, until the virus makes them too sick.

Today, so many people accept those who are affected by the virus and treat them as they would treat any other person in their lives. And yet people, both kids and adults, who are HIV positive or who have developed AIDS have been discriminated against.

Some children, along with their families, are forced to move—only because they are HIV positive or have developed the AIDS virus. Other children are teased or left out of activities.

So, if you know someone who is HIV positive or has developed AIDS, treat that person kindly. Shake hands, say hello, give a hug, talk with that person, and work and play with that person—all these things are safe to do—and treat that person as you would treat any good friend.

28
Staying Healthy
Responsible Choices

A large part of growing up is learning to take care of yourself in a healthy way.

I'm an expert on growing up now. I know a lot!

I know just enough.

Eating healthy foods, exercising almost daily, keeping your body clean, wearing clean clothes, staying away from drugs and alcohol, and having regular medical checkups—all of these things can help you be healthy and stay healthy as you go through puberty.

But there's more to staying healthy than just taking good care of your body. It also means taking responsibility for your own actions—for yourself and for what you do. It means making healthy choices for yourself, including choices about your body and about sex. And it means having respect for yourself and your own decisions.

Staying healthy also involves having healthy relationships with other people. That means not only taking good care of yourself, but also taking good care of your friends. Having a good friend or friends as you grow up can help you learn how to have healthy relationships with other people that involve sharing, caring, and respect for others as well as for yourself.

As you go through life, friendship is a big part of every healthy relationship, whether two people like, love, or like and love each other, whether they choose to be friends, to date, to be partners, or to marry.

Yet puberty is a time when friends, even good friends, often try to persuade or

pressure one another to try out new things. Some of these things, which may involve sex, alcohol, drugs, or going on some online sites, may be things you do not want to do, or are not ready to do, or are afraid to do, or feel are not safe to do. That's when it's important to make the decision that is best for you—one that is safe and healthy for you.

Everyone makes mistakes and has bad judgment once in a while, and you probably will too. But most of the time, you can and will make responsible choices—ones that are good for you, right for you, and healthy for you and your friends.

THANK YOU!

Thank you to each one of you, all experts in your own fields, who continue to be our most trusted sources. Ever since this book was first published, your careful reading of the words and your astute assessment of the artwork helped us to do our best to make sure that the information in this book is up-to-date, medically and scientifically accurate, psychologically appropriate, and age appropriate. In these times, when there are rapid scientific, medical, and cultural changes and a myriad of places to find information about sexual health, we believe that in order to stay healthy, older kids, preteens, and teens deserve to have information that is fact-based and truthful. Thank you for helping us do that and for teaching us so well.

With gratitude, RHH and ME

* Each expert's name and attribution have been taken directly from the *It's Perfectly Normal* edition in which their name was last listed.

Tina Alu, *sexuality education coordinator, Cambridge Family Planning, Cambridge, MA*

Bebe J. Anderson, JD, *director, US Legal Program, Center for Reproductive Rights, New York, NY*

Wendy Apfel, *educational technology coordinator, Bank Street School for Children, New York, NY*

Joan E. Bertin, JD, *executive director, National Coalition Against Censorship, New York, NY*

Sara Birss, MD, *child psychiatrist, developmental pediatrician, Cambridge, MA*

Rosa Casamassima, *consultant, Medford, MA*

Deborah Chamberlain, MA, LMHC, *mental health specialist, Cambridge, MA*

David S. Chapin, MD, *director of gynecology, Beth Israel Hospital, Boston, MA*

Paula and Chuck Collins, *parents, San Francisco, CA*

Edward J. Collins, MD, *assistant clinical professor, University of California at San Francisco, CA*

Eileen M. Costello, MD, *pediatrician; chief of ambulatory pediatrics, Boston Medical Center; clinical professor of pediatrics, Boston University School of Medicine, Boston, MA*

Kirsten Dahl, PhD, *associate professor, Yale University Child Study Center, New Haven, CT*

Gregory David, MA, MSEd, *9/10s head teacher, Bank Street School for Children, New York, NY*

Angela Diaz, MD, MPH, *professor, Department of Pediatrics and Department of Preventative Medicine, Icahn School of Medicine at Mount Sinai, director, Mount Sinai Adolescent Health Center, New York, NY*

Mary Dominguez, *science teacher, Shady Hill School, Cambridge, MA*

Nancy Drooker, *sexuality education consultant, San Francisco, CA*

Amy Ehrlich, *executive editor, Candlewick Press, Cambridge, MA*

Dan Frank, PhD, *principal, Francis W. Parker School, Chicago, IL*

Nicki Nichols Gamble, *past president and CEO, Planned Parenthood of Massachusetts, Boston, MA*

Frieda Garcia, *president, United South End Settlements, Boston, MA*

Judith Gardner, PhD, *psychologist, Brandeis University, Waltham, MA*

Trudy Goodman, MEd, *child and family therapist, Cambridge, MA*

Gerald Haas, MD, *pediatrician, Cambridge, MA; physician in chief, South End Community Health Center, Boston, MA*

Benjamin H. Harris, PhD, *clinical psychologist, Doctoral Program in Clinical Psychology, City College of New York, New York, NY*

David B. Harris, PhD, *child advocate, Children's Research and Education Institute, New York, NY*

Emily B. Harris, MD, *pediatrician, New York, NY*

Hilary G. Harris, *consultant, New York, NY*

William W. Harris, PhD, *child advocate, Children's Research and Education Institute, New York, NY*

Alexandra M. Harrison, MD, *child psychiatrist, child and adult psychoanalyst, Boston Psychoanalytic Society and Institute; Cambridge Health Alliance, Cambridge, MA*

William Haseltine, PhD, *chief, Division of Human Retrovirology, Harvard Medical School, Dana Farber Cancer Institute, Boston, MA*

M. Peter Heilbrun, MD, *chairman, Department of Neurosurgery, University of Utah, Salt Lake City, UT*

Robyn O. Heilbrun, JD, *consultant, Salt Lake City, UT*

Doris B. Held, MEd, *psychotherapist, Harvard Medical School; member of the Governor's Commission on Gay and Lesbian Youth for the Commonwealth of MA, Cambridge, MA*

Lance Hidy, *designer, Boston, MA*

Michael Iskowitz, *chief counsel for poverty, AIDS, and family policy, US Senate Committee on Labor and Human Resources, Washington, DC*

Jennifer Johnsen, MPH, *vice president, digital programs and education, Power to Decide, Washington DC*

Leslie M. Kantor, PhD, MPH, *professor and chair, Department of Urban-Global Public Health, Rutgers School of Public Health, Newark, NJ; former vice president of education, Planned Parenthood Federation of America, New York, NY*

Maureen Kelly, MATD, *vice president for programming and communications, Planned Parenthood of the Southern Finger Lakes, Ithaca, NY*

Larry Kessler, *executive director, AIDS Action Committee of MA, Boston, MA; commissioner, US National Commission on AIDS, Washington, DC*

Robert A. King, MD, *assistant professor of child psychiatry, Yale University Child Study Center, New Haven, CT*

Perri Klass, MD, *professor of journalism and pediatrics, New York University, New York, NY*

Susan Kuklin, *children's book author and photographer, New York, NY*

Elizabeth A. Levy, *children's book author, New York, NY*

Jay A. Levy, MD, *professor, Department of Medicine; affiliate member, Cancer Research Institute; director, Laboratory for Tumor and AIDS Virus Research, University of California School of Medicine, San Francisco, CA*

Leroy Lewis, *teacher, Martin Luther King School, Cambridge, MA*

Fran Linkin, MPH, *director of research, reproductive rights, State Innovation Exchange (SiX), New York, NY*

Ben Lowengard, *digital content consultant, Belmont, MA*

Carol Lynch, *director of counseling, Planned Parenthood Clinic, Brookline, MA*

Mary Mann, *MLIS, author and librarian, Brooklyn, NY*

Michael McGee, *vice president of education, Planned Parenthood Federation of America, New York, NY*

Ted Mermin, *teacher, The Atrium School, Watertown, MA*

Nancy Meyer, *parent, New York, NY*

Ronald James Moglia, EdD, *director, Graduate Program in Human Sexuality, New York University, New York, NY*

Elizabeth Nash, *MPP, senior state issues manager, Guttmacher Institute, Washington DC*

Eli H. Newberger, MD, *pediatrician; founder and medical director, 1970–2000, Child Protection Program, adjunct professor in pediatrics, Boston Children's Hospital, Boston, MA*

Brenda O'Conner, teacher, M E Fitzgerald School, Cambridge, MA

June E. Osborn, MD, dean, School of Public Health, University of Michigan; chairman, US National Commission on AIDS, Washington, DC

J. C. Pankratz, organizational development specialist, Planned Parenthood League of Massachusetts, Boston, MA

Kyle Pruett, MD, clinical professor of psychiatry, Yale University Child Study Center, New Haven, CT

Jeffrey Pudney, PhD, research associate, Harvard Medical School, Boston, MA

Frank W. Putnam, MD, professor of pediatrics and psychiatry, Cincinnati Children's Hospital Medical Center, Cincinnati, OH

Louise Rice, RN, associate director of education, AIDS Action Committee of Massachusetts, Boston, MA

Lourdes Rivera, JD, senior vice president, US Programs, Center for Reproductive Rights, New York, NY

Monica Rodriguez, director of information and education, Sexuality Information and Education Council of the United States, New York, NY

Deborah M. Rothman, sexuality educator, author, Baltimore, MD

Heather Z. Sankey, MD, vice chair for education, Department of Obstetrics and Gynecology, Baystate Medical Center, Springfield, MA

Annabel Sheinberg, MM, vice president of learning and partnerships, Planned Parenthood Association of Utah, Salt Lake City, UT

Rachel Skvirsky, PhD, associate professor of biology, University of Massachusetts, Boston, MA

Jen Slonaker, MSW, chief strategy officer, Planned Parenthood League of Massachusetts, Boston, MA

Priscilla J. Smith, JD, director, Domestic Legal Program, Center for Reproductive Rights, New York, NY

Norman Spack, MD, codirector, Gender Management Service, Endocrine Division, Boston Children's Hospital, Boston, MA

Paula Stahl, EdD, executive director, Children's Charter Trauma Clinic, Waltham, MA

Michael G. Thompson, PhD, clinical psychologist, author, Cambridge, MA

Lawrence H. Tribe, Tyler Professor of Constitutional Law, Harvard Law School, Cambridge, MA

Maeve Visser Knoth, librarian, San Mateo County Library, Atherton, CA

Susan Webber, consultant, Arlington, MA

Rosalind M. Weir, parent, Cambridge, MA

Marc N. Weiss, Web Lab, New York, NY

Ilyon Woo, student, Cambridge, MA

Barry Zuckerman, MD, professor of pediatrics, Boston University School of Medicine, Boston, MA

Pamela Zuckerman, MD, pediatrician, Boston, MA

Thank you to **Cecile Richards,** cofounder, Supermajority; former president, Planned Parenthood Federation of America, for your steadfast support of our work over the years.

Thanks to all our colleagues at Candlewick Press and Walker Books. Another giant thank-you to our editor, **Hilary Van Dusen,** and to editor **Miriam Newman** and designer **Jackie Shepherd** for your continuing commitment to keeping this book current for today's and tomorrow's older kids, preteens, and teens, no matter how much time and work it took to do so.

INDEX

A

abortion, 82–86

abortion pill, 82

abstinence, 59, 61, 62, 75–76, 81, 99, 104

abuse, 93–96

adolescence, 31. *See also* puberty

adoption, 73–74, 84, 85

afterbirth, 69

AIDS (acquired immunodeficiency syndrome), 10, 101–105. *See also* HIV; sexually transmitted diseases; sexually transmitted infections

alcohol, 66, 95, 106, 107

amniotic fluid, 65, 67

amniotic sac, 65, 67, 69

anal intercourse (anal sex), 60, 62, 75, 77, 79, 97, 103

anus, 10, 23, 26, 62, 77

artificial insemination, 72–73

asexual, 13, 14

assisted insemination, 72–73

athletic cup, 46

B

babies, 3, 5, 8–9, 31, 32, 33, 54–55, 61, 63, 72–74

bathrooms, 15–16

binary, 15

biological parents, 56, 57

birth, 25, 38, 42, 67–71

birth canal, 67. *See also* vagina

birth certificate, 3–4

birth control, 9, 61, 62, 76–81. *See also* contraception

birth parents, 56, 57

bisexual, 11, 12, 13, 15

bladder, 27, 41

blood, 23, 25, 35–36, 41, 42. *See also* menstruation

bodies, 1, 3, 5, 18–21, 28–29, 43–44, 45–47, 48

body hair, 43, 44, 45, 48

body odor, 45

bra, 46

breastfeeding, 70, 103–104

breasts, 43, 46, 48

breech birth, 69

bullying, 15, 91–92

C

calendar method (rhythm method), 80. *See also* birth control

cancer, 10, 98, 99, 101

cell phones, 87, 90–92

cells, 56–58, 63, 65. *See also* eggs; sperm

cervical cap, 77, 78, 79. *See also* birth control

cervix, 24, 25, 36, 63, 67, 79, 99

cesarean birth (C-section), 69

checkups, 66, 82, 93, 97, 99–100, 101, 106

chlamydia, 77, 98. *See also* sexually transmitted diseases; sexually transmitted infections

chromosomes, 56–58. *See also* DNA

circumcision, 25, 26, 70

cisgender, 14

climax, 52, 61

clitoris, 22, 23, 51, 60

computers, 87–92

conception, 33, 63, 76

condoms, 62, 76–77, 99, 103, 104

consent, giving, 59–60, 94–95

contraception, 76, 80, 81, 86, 99. *See also* birth control

contraceptives, 77, 78, 79. *See also* birth control; contraception

crabs (pubic lice), 97–98. *See also* sexually transmitted diseases; sexually transmitted infections

cramps, 35

crushes, 6–7, 12, 13

cyberbullying, 92. *See also* bullying

D

Depo-Provera (the shot), 77, 78, 79. *See also* birth control

desire, sexual, 6–7, 11

diaphragm, 77, 78, 79. *See also* birth control

dirty words, 28, 95

diseases, 9, 10, 51, 62, 66, 70, 75, 76, 80, 77, 80, 82, 85, 88, 97–100, 101. *See also* infection; sexually transmitted diseases; sexually transmitted infections

DNA (deoxyribonucleic acid), 56. *See also* chromosomes

drugs, 66, 95, 98, 101, 103, 106, 107

intersex, 3, 58
IUD, 77, 78–79, 80. *See also* birth
control

J

jockstrap, 46
June Medical Services versus Russo, 85.
See also abortion

L

labia, 22, 23, 24
labor, 67
larynx, 44
laws and rulings, 82–86
lesbian, 11, 12–13, 14, 15. *See also*
gay; homosexual
LGBTQ+ (lesbian, gay, bisexual,
transgender, queer/questioning,
plus), 11–16
lice, pubic (crabs), 97–98. *See also*
sexually transmitted diseases;
sexually transmitted infections

M

making love, 8–10, 59–62. *See also*
sexual intercourse
male, 2, 3, 11–15, 41, 43, 44, 52, 59,
61, 62, 72, 73, 76, 77, 79, 80
marriage, 16, 106
masturbation, 51–52
menopause, 35
menstrual cup, 23, 36
menstruation, 25, 34–38, 43
midwife, 3, 67, 69, 78
miscarriage (spontaneous abortion),
86
moods, 32, 50. *See also* feelings

morning-after pills, 79–80. *See also*
emergency contraception
multiple birth, 57

N

navel, 66
needles, 98, 103, 104
nipples, 43, 44
nocturnal emission, 42. *See also* wet
dream
non-binary, 15
nurse, 67

O

Obergefell versus Hodges (same-sex
marriage), 16
online, 41, 46, 76, 78, 79, 80, 87–92
opioids, 66. *See also* drugs
oral intercourse (oral sex), 60, 62, 77
organs, 5, 13, 22–27, 57, 65. *See also*
reproductive organs; sex organs
orgasm, 41, 52, 61
ova, 24. *See also* eggs
ovaries, 5, 24, 32, 33, 34, 35, 39, 43,
44, 72, 78, 79, 80
over-the-counter birth control, 76,
79, 80
ovulation, 33, 80

P

pads, 35–36, 37
pangender, 15
pansexual, 13
Pap smear, 99
patch, the, 77, 78–79. *See also* birth
control

penis, 3, 5, 8, 10, 25–26, 27, 39–42,
44, 45, 46, 48, 51, 60–61, 62, 64,
70, 76
period, 25, 34–38. *See also*
menstruation
pill, the, 77, 78, 79. *See also* birth
control
pimples (zits), 46, 88
placenta, 65–66, 69
plus, 13
pornography, 89
postponement, 59, 75, 76
preemie (premature baby), 70–71
pregnancy, 9, 10, 35, 38, 42, 43, 44,
61, 62, 63–66, 72, 73, 75–81,
82–86, 97, 103
premature baby (preemie), 70–71
prescriptions, 46, 66, 77, 78, 79, 80
privacy, 90–91
private parts, 93
progesterone, 33. *See also* hormones
pronouns, 15
prostate gland, 27, 39, 40, 41.
See also semen
puberty, 30–52
pubic bone, 45
pubic hair, 45
pubic lice (crabs), 97–98. *See also*
sexually transmitted diseases;
sexually transmitted infections

Q

queer, 13
questioning, 13

R

rape, 79, 82, 94, 95
religion, 26, 32, 70, 80, 92, 101

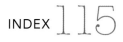

To my husband, to my kids, to Val. Giant thanks!
To Sam, Ella, Daisy, Rosie—my toughest critics,
who keep teaching me what older kids, preteens, and teens
want and need to know. And to their parents.
RHH

To my parents
ME

The designs of the BIRD and the BEE are trademarks of BIRD Productions, Inc. and BEE Productions, Inc.

It's Perfectly Normal is the trademark of BEE Productions, Inc. and BIRD Productions, Inc.

Text copyright © 1994, 2004, 2009, 2014, 2021 by BEE Productions, Inc.
Illustrations copyright © 1994, 2004, 2009, 2014, 2021 by BIRD Productions, Inc.

Fifth edition 2021

Library of Congress Catalog Card Number 2009008457

ISBN 978-1-56402-199-1 (first hardcover edition)
ISBN 978-0-7636-2610-5 (second hardcover edition)
ISBN 978-0-7636-4483-3 (third hardcover edition)
ISBN 978-0-7636-6871-6 (fourth hardcover edition)
ISBN 978-1-5362-0720-0 (fifth hardcover edition)

ISBN 978-1-56402-159-5 (first paperback edition)
ISBN 978-0-7636-2433-0 (second paperback edition)
ISBN 978-0-7636-4484-0 (third paperback edition)
ISBN 978-0-7636-6872-3 (fourth paperback edition)
ISBN 978-1-5362-0721-7 (fifth paperback edition)

21 22 23 24 25 26 APS 10 9 8 7 6 5 4 3 2

Printed in Humen, Dongguan, China

This book was typeset in Stempel Schneidler and Journal.
The illustrations were done in watercolor and pencil.

Candlewick Press
99 Dover Street
Somerville, Massachusetts 02144

www.candlewick.com

A FAMILY LIBRARY

A book for every age that answers nearly every question about birth, babies, bodies, families, and healthy sexuality by the award-winning team of Robie H. Harris and Michael Emberley.

MILLIONS of kids have read these books!

Yep! MILLIONS of kids around the whole wide world!

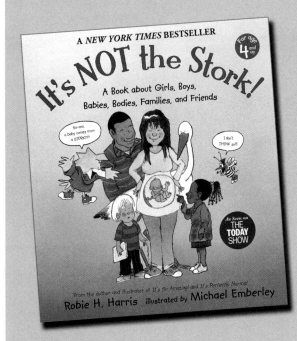

It's NOT the Stork!

helps answer those endless and perfectly normal questions that preschool, kindergarten, and early elementary school children ask about how they began and what makes a girl a girl and a boy a boy.

"An amazingly clear and comprehensive . . . introductory course on the birds and bees. This must-have family resource . . . is reassuring, accurate, up-to-date, and age-appropriate." —*San Francisco Chronicle*

For age **4** *and up*

It's So Amazing!

provides accurate, unbiased answers to nearly every conceivable question about reproduction, birth, and babies, while giving children a healthy understanding of their bodies.

"Even if your child hasn't reached puberty, talk with him or her about what lies ahead. . . . *It's So Amazing!* . . . could help prepare your son or daughter—as well as reassure you."

—*Time* Magazine

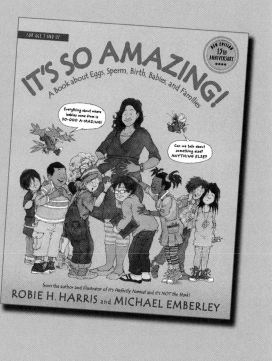

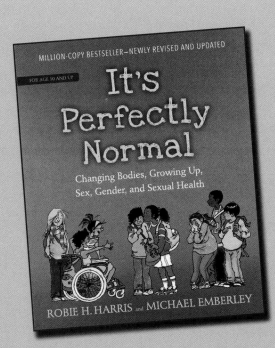

It's Perfectly Normal

offers young people the real information they need to make responsible decisions that can help them stay healthy as they approach and experience puberty and adolescence.

"This refreshingly candid tour of the facts of life is just the ticket for jittery parents when it's time to explain the birds and the bees to their curious kids."

—*People* Magazine

For age **10** *and up*

Robie H. Harris

began her career as a teacher at the Bank Street College of Education's School for Children. Her interest in child development issues and the experience of being a parent made her realize "how difficult but necessary it is to talk with children and teenagers about sex and answer questions about this complicated topic. I wanted my kids to stay healthy, so I had to give them accurate information. When I was writing this book, consultations with young people, parents, educators, librarians, doctors, nurses, psychologists, scientists, and clergypeople confirmed the need to educate our young people about sexual health." Robie H. Harris has received Planned Parenthood Federation of America's highest education award—the Mary Lee Tatum Award. This annual award is given to the person who most exemplifies the qualities of an ideal sexuality educator. She is also the author of *It's NOT the Stork!* and *It's So Amazing!*, both illustrated by Michael Emberley, as well as *Who Has What?*, *Who's In My Family?*, *What's In There?*, and *What's So Yummy?* Robie H. Harris lives in New York City.

Michael Emberley,

the son of children's book illustrator Ed Emberley, attended the Rhode Island School of Design. He has been writing and illustrating award-winning books for children for more than thirty years. His titles include *It's NOT the Stork!* and *It's So Amazing!*—both written by Robie H. Harris. About his collaboration with her on *It's Perfectly Normal*, he says, "We felt the same way about the subject from the beginning. Both of us have a strong belief in spreading healthy information rather than hiding it." Michael Emberley lives in Ireland.